Praise for *Languages of Loss*

'Sasha's generosity in writing this vivid, searing account of the loss of her beloved Bill left me deeply moved, moved by the glory of loving and being loved. Her description of moving through the chaos of grief, fully exposing the unknowable inner world of the griever alongside philosophical, spiritual and therapeutic musings were highly illuminating and provocative. But what I was really left with was an awe, an awe of humanity's fundamental and beautiful capacity for loving connection, with one another and with one's self. I will keep this book close to me, always.'

Ed Simons, Psychotherapist and Chemical Brother

'Sasha writes exquisitely and honestly, the sheer rawness of what she has gone through, and is still going through, sitting in balance with the calm and clear-sighted objectivity of the therapist, who is also her. That I so vividly recognise the Bill I knew is testimony to her skill at characterisation – but whether one knew the man or not, one recognises love when one reads it and one recognises the chaotic agony of a love lost. Exploring the threads of her bereavement with such candour and wit and lightness of touch is a remarkable achievement. Bursting through the bitter darkness of her personal experience shine truths that will serve as bright points of light for those who have shared, or are perhaps just embarking upon, the confusing journey of grief.'

Hugh Bonneville

'This is a book fluent not just in the languages of loss but of compassion, humour, empathy, understanding, revelation and humanity. Even in the depths of her own grief Sasha Bates makes sense of the chaos that envelops all of us and offers not a reductive path to some kind of quasi-redemption but the profound glimpse of a way through.'

Tim Marlow, writer and broadcaster

Languages of Loss

A Psychotherapist's Journey Through Grief

SASHA BATES

First published in Great Britain in 2020 by Yellow Kite
An imprint of Hodder & Stoughton
An Hachette UK company

1

A CIP catalogue record for this title is available from the British Library

Hardback ISBN 978 1 529 31269 0
eBook ISBN 978 1 529 31418 2

Typeset in Minion Pro by Hewer Text UK Ltd, Edinburgh
Printed and bound in Great Britain by Clays Ltd, Elcograf S.p.A.

Hodder & Stoughton policy is to use papers that are natural, renewable
and recyclable products and made from wood grown in sustainable
forests. The logging and manufacturing processes are expected to
conform to the environmental regulations of the country of origin.

Yellow Kite
Hodder & Stoughton Ltd
Carmelite House
50 Victoria Embankment
London EC4Y 0DZ

www.yellowkitebooks.co.uk

For Billy

'Night had settled, and the train windows were now half-opaque, so you could choose whether to look out the window into the dark landscape outside, or keep your focus on the reflection back into the train carriage. I've always liked that trick of perspective and perception. I alternated between the reflection and the view through the window.'

The Wall, John Lanchester

Foreword

'We die. That may be the meaning of life.
But we do language. That may be the measure of our lives.'

Toni Morrison

I met Billy Cashmore in 1992 when I played his wife in a little known Feydeau farce called *No Flies on Mr Hunter!* He played the philandering eponymous title role. We both agreed that we weren't very good in it (Billy said 'rubbish', one of his favourite words) and I struggled to keep a straight face on stage from the moment I met him. Billy was a very funny man, full of wit and silliness, smart observation and searing insight into the nonsense humans get up to. He was also loyal, trustworthy, compassionate, generous, encouraging, complex and incredibly kind. I loved him as a true friend and there began a friendship of twenty-five years until his sudden death.

Three months before I got married in 1997, Bill phoned me up to say he'd won a round-the-world trip as a frequent user of the then BT chargecard, and did I want to accompany him? My husband-to-be agreed that it was – as it was pitched to Billy by the good people of BT – a trip of a lifetime, and to be embraced. We spent a hilarious and enlightening three weeks in Singapore, Bali, Hawaii and Los Angeles.

Then Billy met Sasha. He adored her and cherished her and gave thanks for her all the time. Life with Sasha was the real trip of a lifetime he had always been waiting for.

Billy and Sasha travelled extensively together, embracing the adventure of otherness, and rejoicing in each other's company. They were also both travel journalists, expertly recording their experiences and perspectives for various publications. They collected and curated travelling encounters with relish and delightful humour. Bill was also a published writer of plays, sketches, one-man shows and articles. He was a prolific sender of letters and postcards, written in his signature miniature handwriting, always eye-opening, wildly entertaining. In Toni Morrison's words, he 'did language' – he loved the power and necessity of words as a moment-to-moment legacy of lives fully lived.

And then Bill died.

It doesn't seem a possible thing. I don't like to write it. I can't imagine a world where Billy Cashmore isn't present, commenting with his piercing trademark accuracy on the ludicrous and the beautiful. I don't want Sasha to have lost him. I hate the fact that she has had to write this book. This book shouldn't have needed to be written.

But here it is. It is a vivid, candid dialogue between Sasha's internal characters, with two standout roles topping the bill. Part memoir, part analysis, it takes us on an unforgettable journey into the heart of grief. It may be Billy and Sasha's finest travel journalism to date. At times unbearably sad, at others profoundly insightful, it is never anything less than intensely honest, personal and illuminating.

Sasha and Billy both 'do language' to measure out the shape of their days. This book, like all healing, contains immeasurable pain, yet the common thread that runs through it is not desolation, but hope. Perhaps language, for Sasha, is giving both measure and meaning to help her, and us, navigate tempestuous waters.

I know that I will give this book to many people, to those who are grieving, and those who stand alongside grief in all its various guises. I will most probably give it with a health warning:

'This book may very well be good for your health.'

Tamsin Greig
August 2019

Prologue

This book is my attempt to make sense of what the hell happened to me one year ago, when the man I'd waited thirty-five years to meet, the man I loved more than anything in the world, a man training for his third marathon, a vegetarian, Quaker, non-smoking, moderate drinking, seemingly fighting fit and healthy 56-year-old with everything to live for, stopped living. And to acknowledge how part of me stopped living along with him. I lost my partner, best friend, lover, soulmate, companion, and I also lost my future. I lost a huge chunk of myself. I lost the ground beneath my feet. I lost hope. I lost the will to live.

And yet here I am, one year on, writing a book, clearly surviving (well, alive), and, externally at least, thriving. How have I got from there to here? Well, part of that journey consists of telling this story – the story of how I am getting through the sudden death of my adored husband. Not getting over it – that is too much to ask – but getting through it, learning how to live with it, learning how to make space for it, how to rearrange myself around it. Learning how to cope with the shock, denial, anger, depression – all those supposedly nice, clean, clearly defined (ha!) stages we have been told grief consists of.

Stupidly I thought I knew quite a lot about these stages – and other theories about how to manage grief – already. Because – and here's the kicker – I actually counsel grieving people for a living. I'm a psychotherapist. I've read, and studied, and worked with grief for years. I've sat with countless others going through it, trying to help them find ways to manage their own expressions of grief.

So does any of this knowledge and experience help me deal with my own grief? Does my training help lessen the excruciating pain or provide a language with which to render the incomprehensible comprehensible?

Having been unwillingly obliged, in the most brutal way, to marry theory and practice, I can now reflect on what, during that terrible first year, my two selves had to go through: my 'grieving self' and my 'therapist self'. Maybe their combined lived experience and academic knowledge might offer a little bit of insider understanding to others going through a bereavement, or to their friends who want to help, but don't know how. It may even have something for those who come into contact with bereaved people through their work – doctors, social workers, undertakers, or even, like me, therapists who know the theory but haven't yet experienced it in person.

From within the rawness of the experience 'grieving me' will tell you what happened to my husband the actor, writer, director and entrepreneur Bill Cashmore, and how losing him feels. 'Therapist me' will observe and offer a professional perspective on the various theories surrounding grief, exploring how they intersect with the wider psychotherapeutic approaches that have emerged over the years, all the ways we have found to help us understand ourselves better – from

Freud to existentialism, transpersonal therapy to body psychotherapy, and more. Most importantly I want to learn as much as I can about this all-too-common experience – one that not one of us will ever avoid, much as we avoid talking about it. Avoiding things, 'therapist me' knows all too well, never ends well. So, let's not allow 'grieving me' to dodge telling this story, however much she might not want to return to that agonising first year.

Chapter One

Implosion

'And there you have the cause of Brexit, right there'.

It is a funny time to be discussing Brexit, but to be fair, Jess *is* trying to be funny. Which in itself is rather funny, because most people don't make black jokes about Brexit, or anything else, at the bedside of their best friend's husband as he lies dying in a coma in hospital. But if there is one thing I am discovering about grief, it is that a sense of humour is not only desirable, but completely essential to survival. Or at least for me it is, and grief is nothing if not individually tailored. Jess, who has known me for thirty-two years, knows that. Just as she knows that it is my husband Bill's hilarious offbeat humour that first attracted me to him, and is what has kept me laughing with him, interested in him, loving him and admiring him still, fourteen years on from the day we met. He is my life and it is inconceivable that I can survive without him. But apparently that is exactly what I am expected to do.

Two days ago, on an ordinary Sunday in November, Bill and I were eating breakfast in our house in Shepherd's Bush. A couple of hours later, as the paramedic lifted Bill into the ambulance, he asked me what the last thing was that Bill had eaten.

'Kale omelette with avocado and sourdough,' I am forced to reveal. 'Please don't hate us.'

It was hearing me tell this embarrassing tale of West London, middle-class, middle-aged pretentiousness that caused Jess's definitive analysis of why the rest of the country hates London elites so much. It is also her way of trying to make me laugh as Bill lies wired up to the machines that are keeping him alive.

Can you tell I'm avoiding recounting the events that led to our being there at his hospital bedside? I am trying to explain things honestly, but even now, a year on, my brain struggles to return to those early days without shutting down or turning to humour and distraction activities so as not to think too deeply about the day my life imploded.

So, let's drag my reluctant mind back there, back to our Brexit-inducing breakfast of kale omelette, avocado and sourdough that we are munching through as we discuss our plans for the day. We are due to meet our friends, Tim and Tanya, for lunch at a new restaurant in town, but before then are going to head to our usual Sunday Quaker Meeting. Bill's been training hard for his third marathon but still wants a bit of light exercise, so we decide to walk the couple of miles to the Meeting House, so we can jump on the tube into town for our lunch straight after. Such are the mundanities of shared life that seem so insignificant at the time but which not only take on huge significance when you realise that is the last proper conversation you will ever have, but also deliver acute pangs of pain when you think back. Think back to how easy and comfortable life is when you get to share it with your best friend and soulmate. And how different life alone is; breakfasting alone is; planning your day alone is.

We finish breakfast where, as usual, he cleared because I'd cooked – more casual easiness – and we wander upstairs to get dressed, continuing to chat about inconsequential things as I put on my make-up and Bill chooses one of the three new shirts he'd bought the weekend before. He loathed shopping and I was lucky to get him in a shop more than once a year, so when I managed it, and he found something he liked, I made sure he bought several at once so as to delay for a bit longer the next bout of annoyed and annoying griping about the need to go shopping.

He lays the shirt out on the bed, leans down to pull off the label, then suddenly screams and stands upright, clutching his chest.

Bill had been an actor throughout his twenties. He started his own communications and training business in his thirties, but the acting instinct had never migrated far from the surface, and I had become used to very melodramatic outbursts over the tiniest things. I'd learned to develop selective hearing and to dampen down my startle response after too many years of rushing downstairs at top speed in response to a blood-curdling yell of pain or anger, only to find he'd stuck a stamp on the wrong way up or couldn't find a particular mug. But this, I know immediately, is different. This is real.

The look on his face is terrifying. He looks like he's seen a ghost: he's white, shocked, glazed, confused, frightened and clearly in massive pain. Because the pain had come on as he bent over, my first thought is that he has slipped a disc, something he's done once before when bending and twisting at a funny angle. But it is his chest he's clutching, and his breathing is laboured.

He is moaning and wide-eyed and I have no idea what to do.

'Are you having a heart attack?' I ask, clearly not very helpfully, but I am panicking. 'Can you speak?'

I stare at his face, dredging my mind for what I think could be signs of a stroke – would it mean his face was asymmetrical? Am I meant to ask him to lift his left arm or something? Shit, why is this stuff so hard to remember? Now he's holding his neck and saying that hurts, too.

'Should I call an ambulance? Should I drive you to the urgent care centre?'

Asking his opinion comes as second nature. We are such a good team, Bill and I; we make all our decisions communally, refer to each other for advice, so I can't not see this as a decision to take together, but he is clearly in no fit state to have an opinion. I don't know what to do. He isn't talking but is still upright and now he is clutching his groin.

'Ouuww. It hurts here too,' he gasps.

'Sit down, I think I should drive you to Hammersmith, can you get your shirt and shoes on?'

My mind is all over the place. Is this bad enough to call an ambulance? What is happening? How can he go from having a pain in the chest, to in the neck, then in the groin? What the hell is this? Not knowing whether to call an ambulance is part classic British response – not wanting to overreact and be THAT person who wastes the time of the emergency services unnecessarily – and part practicality – we live just five minutes' drive from Hammersmith Hospital's urgent care centre and we know this because Bill has had to whizz me up there a couple of times – once when I'd had 'avocado hand', and once just a few weeks ago after I'd had shoulder surgery and the wound had opened up, causing our bed to look like a murder scene. I am only recently out of the sling and have the use of both arms for the first time in several weeks. And thank God I do, because I now take the unilateral decision that driving him to Hammersmith myself will be the quicker option. With some difficulty I help him into his shirt and a pair of shoes, and we limp out of the house.

I don't know it then, but Bill will never again cross this threshold, will never return to this home we've created together. I will never again be walking out the front door as one half of a couple. In fact, this will be the last time we will ever do anything as a couple. My return will be to another world: opening the door to an empty house, alone, my life and future eviscerated in a puff of smoke, all certainties destroyed.

Just thirty-six hours after that ridiculous, now (to me) legendary, breakfast, I will hear the words, 'I'm sorry, there's nothing more we can do.'

~

I drive up the road towards Hammersmith Hospital, the five-minute journey feeling like twenty, and still with my mind racing and darting about between two weird parallel states, one part wondering if we are overreacting, another part really scared and wondering whether I should just floor it and risk 'my husband was in great pain' being a good enough excuse to get me off any resulting speeding fines. What if it turns out to be indigestion? Or trapped wind? But what is going on with the leg thing, the groin thing, the pins and needles that are the latest weird manifestation of whatever it is that is happening here? What can it be? What on earth connects this plethora of disjointed symptoms? I am really scared. I've never seen Bill, or anyone, like this.

We arrive, Bill is taken into triage and his vital signs measured and noted. He is now complaining of blurred vision and nausea as well. We are told to wait back out in the waiting room, but his left leg has become so numb he needs a wheel-chair to get him there.

We sit, we wait, and I frantically google 'stroke symptoms', 'slipped disc symptoms' and 'heart attack symptoms' – the three most likely scenarios I can think of. I keep up a trying-to-be-reassuring running commentary as I do so: 'I don't think it's a stroke my love, and the nurse didn't mention a heart attack. I think it's muscular, I think you've trapped a nerve in your spine and it's having odd side effects.' I cling to my ill-informed diagnosis as it is the least terrifying to contemplate. Bill sits quietly, still breathing heavily and clearly in pain.

I go and try to rustle up a bit more of a sense of urgency from the receptionist: 'I think this is serious, can you get the doctor to see him now, please?' I ask, really far more scared than my soothing babbling to him lets on.

'She has someone with her, but he's next in line,' I'm told; 'the other patient also needs help.'

'I need the loo,' says Bill on my return.

I wheel him to the loo, then leave him to sort himself out while I hover outside the door waiting for him to come out. Very soon I hear a cry that he can't get off the loo. I go in and try to help him back into the chair, but it is apparent that he has lost all feeling and use of his left leg and I'm not strong enough to help, so he falls to the floor, moaning. I start shouting for help and suddenly several people are there with me to help him. Now they start taking us seriously. More nurses arrive, get him out of the loo and onto a bed and start wiring him up to various devices.

I am ushered in to see the doctor, who asks me yet again – I've already recounted his symptoms over and over to receptionist, triage nurse, emergency nurses – what exactly happened. Again, I list the mad collection of ailments – first it was his chest, then his neck, then his groin, then pins and needles in his left leg, then blurred vision, feeling sick, numbness in his leg, stomach pains, finally paralysis of his leg. The doctor is looking bemused and panicked. I do not at all like the sight of a bemused and panicked doctor. She rings a colleague in the cardiology department and asks her to look at the results of the heart rate tests they took in triage, seemingly convinced that it must have been some sort of heart attack. But none of it makes sense. It's slightly more understandable that it makes no sense to me, but she is equally baffled. I am getting more and more scared. She keeps saying she doesn't understand what it could be and asks me yet again to tell her the sequence of events. At this point she is running to and fro between me in the consulting room, and Bill on the bed in the emergency area – an area I have been banned from while they do the wiring up and various tests. I have no idea how much time passes, probably only fifteen minutes or so, but it feels longer; then the doctor says to one of the nurses: 'I just don't know, I think we should call an ambulance, shall I call an ambulance? Yes, I think I'm going to call an ambulance.'

My sense of the surreal deepens. Aren't we already in hospital? Isn't she a doctor? Why are we calling an ambulance from a hospital? What the hell is happening? Am I dreaming? Please let me be dreaming. This is all too bloody odd.

An ambulance arrives and I feel reassured by the calm air of competence emitted by the paramedic. I am yet to confess to my middle-class elitism re the breakfast, so he still likes me at this point and explains that we are going down to Charing Cross Hospital where the accident and emergency department with its MRI scanner resides.

Bill is wheeled out on the gurney and into the ambulance and I squeeze his hand and tell him everything is under control. It seems that Hammersmith Hospital, having had its A and E department downgraded to Urgent Care, is pretty much just a glorified GP surgery, and the doctor we saw was a GP, clearly unused to emergencies of Bill's type – whatever on earth Bill's type is. We are still to find out as we rush – lights flashing, siren blaring from Hammersmith to Charing Cross Hospital. Bill is screaming in pain and I keep up a reassuring tone as I tell him of our progress: 'We're nearly there my darling, we're just approaching Hammersmith roundabout so not long now. You're going to be fine. Look, now we're leaving the roundabout so we're practically there, it can't be more than a minute now, and as soon as we are, they will scan you and we will know what is going on and then we can sort it out. You're going to be fine my darling.'

On arrival Bill is whisked away and I am asked who I am. I feel I've been pretty cool, calm and collected till now – externally at least – but as I open my mouth to tell them 'I'm his wife' the words stick, my voice breaks and I start to wobble. I realise I am not as okay as I thought I was – my first indication in the moment of how in times of trauma body and mind really do go their separate ways in order to help a person survive massive shock.

I am led to a 'family room', a tiny empty box containing three uncomfortable chairs and a table, and am left there alone for what, again, feels like a very, very long time. My body starts to shake. I can tell I am in shock. I feel cold and frightened by my inability to control the convulsions causing my body to act independently of my mind. I can hear Bill's screams of pain from down the corridor. They chill me to the bone, and part of me notes the literalness of this expression. I want to be with him but do not know exactly where they have taken him and don't trust my own legs enough to go and search.

More time passes. I don't know what to do with myself. I decide to ring a friend but am worried about disturbing her Sunday and interrupting a happy family day with my terrible worrying news, or rather non-news, as I still don't know what is going on. I text her instead: 'are you in the middle of something?' No response. Long minutes go by. I send the same text to another friend, realising I really do need to talk to someone or I will go mad. No response again. I text my mother – 'Bill has collapsed, we don't know why. I'm in the hospital with him while they run some tests.' She immediately texts back

– 'I'm on my way.' I feel relieved. I feel I have done something productive and so mitigated a tiny part of the terrifying help-lessness overwhelming me.

I text the friends we were meant to be meeting for lunch to tell them we can't make it. I text my clients and cancel them all for this week, just in case. I don't yet know it, but this is just the start of what will be hours and days of calls and texts and emails, all cancelling and rearranging and informing and planning – friends, family, work, hobbies, planned holidays – all these things need to be sorted out.

After an age I decide I ought to eat something as it is now past lunchtime. I am scared to leave this hellhole of a family room in case I miss someone coming with news, but I also feel I will go mad if I stay here much longer. I roam the corridors look-ing for the hospital shop, where I buy a banana, a coffee and a copy of the *Observer*, starting what is going to prove to be another essential act over the coming year – looking for distraction in any shape or form.

Back in the family room, coffee drunk, part of the banana eaten, *Observer* pictures glanced at, a doctor arrives.

'It is what I told you before, it's what we thought it was, an aortic dissection.'

What had she told me before? Did I have a conversation with this woman? I have no recollection of her telling me any of this, although she does look vaguely familiar from our arrival, when seemingly hundreds of people converged on us and whisked Bill away. Maybe she was the one who asked who I was and led me to the family room – God, what has happened to my brain, all this happened probably less than an hour ago and yet I can't put the faces or events or what I've been told in any sort of order. I need to focus.

'What the hell is an aortic dissection,' I ask, 'and what do we do about it?'

'Well, first we are going to take you back to Hammersmith.'

'What? Why? We've only just come from Hammersmith, why are we going back there?'

'You had to come here because this is where the MRI scanner is kept, but Hammersmith is where the cardiology department is, so we need to get you back there in an ambulance. He needs urgent heart surgery. The surgeon has been notified and is making his way there now too.'

Whoa! Okay. Heart surgery sounds serious.

Clearly this is not a moment to dwell on the political ramifications of how austerity, years of starving the NHS of funds and the systematic closing down of A and E departments has led to this ridiculous to- and fro-ing across London in various ambulances, wasting precious minutes that could have potentially saved his life. I know better than to go down that rabbit hole. In the moment I am more concerned with just retracing our steps, and with trying to understand what an aortic dissection is.

Back in the ambulance – in the front this time as there is a team of people gathered around Bill behind and no room for me – I again start googling, having understood nothing of what the kind doctor had been trying to explain to me.

Bill is quiet now and I keep calling back to him over my shoulder that it's going to be fine. 'We have to go to see a different doctor, now, back at Hammersmith. He knows what to do.'

I think that I've understood what they've told me about what's going on, or at least I've gleaned bits and pieces from them, and from Wikipedia and other websites.

I learn that Bill's aorta, the largest artery in the body, the one that pumps blood away from the heart, has split, causing the blood that is usually contained therein to run amok and make its way to other parts of the body where it has no business being. Clearly that is my layperson's take on an extremely complicated medical phenomenon, but it is all I can manage to cope with. The surgery to come will apparently mend the tear and all will be okay again.

With horrible déjà vu we again race our way across Hammersmith roundabout, in the opposite direction this time, and charge up Shepherds Bush Road and Wood Lane. One of the friends I texted earlier calls me back, but I tell her I will have to ring her later. I call Bill's sister and leave a message about his upcoming surgery. I text Bill's business partner and tell her to cancel all Bill's clients for the coming week. Ridiculously, a part of me is still worried that people will think I am overreacting. It all feels hectic. But at least sorting out practicalities gives me something to do.

On arrival we have a similar scenario to that at Charing Cross, in that armies of people appear and rush us through long corridors and up in lifts, Bill on the gurney, me trotting along beside, trying to hold his hand and talk to him. He has been very quiet but now he whispers: 'What have I got, what are they going to do?' I realise that in all the confusion none of us has actually explained anything to him, or maybe we have but, like me, he has taken none of it in or forgotten it. I tell him as much as I have understood, adding that he is now about to be prepped for surgery while we wait for the surgeon – whoever is unlucky enough to be on call on this no longer quite so quiet Sunday – to abandon his Sunday roast and rush over to us.

We get to ICU and are again separated. I am led to another waiting room by a kind nurse who holds my arm and asks if I would like a hot drink. Again, the veneer of holding it all together cracks in the face of someone being kind to me, someone acknowledging that I am also going through something here. I start to cry, and she sits me down and brings me a cup of tea. Soon I am allowed back to see Bill and one of the many medical staff flying around announces himself as the assistant surgeon and says that he needs to talk to us.

'This is a very serious operation, but he will die without it. If he has it, there is a risk of stroke, and a risk he may not make it.'

My instinctive reaction is fury – what is this stupid man doing, scaring us like that. Bill is about to have a major operation, he needs reassurance not scaremongering, who trained this idiot? Doesn't he know anything about bedside manner?

'I'm going to make it,' croaks Bill.

'Of course you are darling, what an idiot that guy is.'

At this point, for me at least, and, I pray, for Bill also, the thought that he might not make it is complete fantasy, like being told a meteor might strike the Earth. At no point does it cross my mind that the doctor might be right, might be telling me something it is important for me to hear. I just want to give him a piece of my mind for what I see as his bungling insensitivity. I am completely and utterly convinced that Bill will be fine, and my brain will not let even an ounce of doubt shake that conviction. At the time I assume that Bill feels the same; but what happens next now haunts and horrifies me as it makes me wonder if whether, at some level, he did know, that he was in fact more tethered to the reality of the situation than I was.

The doctor comes back with the consent form for the operation. Nowadays you pretty much have to sign your life away just to download a song from iTunes, so I am still assuming this is all just routine and not an indicator of any real danger. Bill is flat on his back and the doctor and I are on either side of the bed, basically talking over his prostrate body. The consent form hovers over Bill's chest and I move to sign it, assuming Bill is too weak to do so.

'I'll do it,' he gasps, raising his head from the pillow just enough to grab the pen and shakily scrawl something that looks nothing like his normal, neat handwriting.

Looking back, I wonder if he was deliberately stopping me from being the one to put my signature to the document that would ultimately make me responsible for these crucial decisions, thus saving me from any residual guilt that might have come in the wake of it. If so, he was protecting me and looking out for me to the very end, and thinking that, my heart feels like it will break. It is also just too painful for me to stay with the corollary thought – that despite his brave words he knew, or suspected, he might not make it. If I'd known he was thinking in those terms I wish he could have voiced it, that we could have talked about that, that he had had a chance to express those fears, that I could have held him and been with him in his fear. Instead, if that is what he was thinking, then he swallowed it down, staying brave on my behalf, and I just cannot bear that. It's not that we didn't say goodbye, we did, but in a 'see you soon' sort of a way that feels so inadequate now.

'I love you very, very much and I will be here when you wake up,' I promise him.

'I love you very, very much too,' he replies.

They wheel him down to the anaesthetic room. He is gone for a few moments and then a doctor comes back and tells me I can go with him. I have a flicker of doubt – not sure that's normal, is it? Do they normally let you go that far? Aren't I meant to wait here? Is there a reason they want me to be with him right up to the point they put him under? But, again, I push that thought away.

I reach the anaesthetic room, tell him as cheerily as I can muster: 'Me back again, come to tell you I love you once more. I'm going to pop off home and feed the cats and charge my phone and I will be here when you wake up.'

He tells me he loves me too as the anaesthetic starts to take effect and he goes under.

It is the last thing he will ever say to me.

~

The first thing Bill ever said to me was, not surprisingly, 'Hello,' quickly followed by 'aren't you going to eat that ice cream?' It was July 2003, the place was Skyros, Greece, and we were finishing up a meal at the communal tables this holistic holiday centre favoured. I was thirty-five and a television director, taking a break before my next job – directing *Grand Designs* for C4. Bill was forty-two, a playwright, a former actor, and the owner of a business training and consulting company specialising in communication. He was taking his first proper holiday in a decade. We were both holidaying alone, each of us having had this place recommended by friends.

I was in a pretty bad place emotionally. I'd just had a terrible break-up and had proceeded to pretty much break down – crying every day and vowing never to get involved with another man ever again.

When Bill announced his arrival in my life by asking for my unwanted ice cream I had no idea he was going to figure in it even peripherally, let alone become the most important thing in it. Yet mere days later, at another communal meal, I realised I was crying again, only this time I was shocked to discover I was crying from laughter, not pain. Out of nowhere it appeared that an angel, manifesting as a middle-aged, overweight Midlander in unfashionable shorts, was shining some light into my darkness with a silly joke.

Within a week, and way out of character for both of us, Bill had scooped up the broken specimen I had become, declared he knew how to love me and look after me, and brought me back to life. Even more surprisingly – I allowed and wanted him to. This was a version of myself I had never met before and it was very disorientating. And incredibly lovely.

And it got even weirder. That very same week that I met Bill I was exchanging contracts on a new house in Shepherd's Bush. By the time of completion six weeks later we had decided that Bill would buy half of it with me and move in. My friends and family thought I'd taken leave of my senses selling half my new house to a strange man I had met in Greece six weeks earlier. But neither of *us* ever had a moment's doubt about whether we were doing the right thing. From that initial burst of unexpected laughter, via a rapid, reckless romance on a Greek beach, we knew we were in this for life. And what a life of travel and exploration we proceeded to have: a lifestyle symbolising our relationship – unconditional love and respect, combining stability with adventure.

The circumstances of our meeting always felt written in the stars – we came from the same city, actually moved in the same social circles, even had six mutual friends, none of whom had ever thought to introduce us. Instead it took a random decision on both our parts to go to the same island on the same day before our meeting could occur. Bill was exhausted after a decade of unceasing work building up his company and had only just allowed himself a holiday, while my recent break-up had put me in a particular state of mind that led to me being more open and uncharacteristically vulnerable. It was a conflation of events that made us able to connect at a far deeper level than might have occurred at any other time or in any other place. It felt like fate. As if it was 'meant to be'. Not being a romantic person, I struggled with this interpretation, yet it felt hard to contradict the signs. God, was I becoming soft?

It certainly seemed as though being with Bill was softening me up, in ways both character-shifting and beyond. Until his arrival in my life, I had definitely tended towards the practical, factual, pragmatic. Bill was the dreamer, the poet, the romantically inclined, affectionate one. In the early years of our relationship he would text me several times a day saying things like: 'I love you,' 'Are you having a nice day?', 'What are you up to?', 'See you soon.' Nice, little, thinking-about-you, not very important but warm and fuzzy, check-in type messages that are so lovely to receive. But such a time-waster to send! I, on the other hand, being a slave to efficacy and productive use of time, was more likely to text him once a week asking: 'Can you get milk?'

I soon learned that relationships need a tiny bit more work than I was putting in, so yes I softened, noticing not just that I was becoming slightly nicer by osmosis and proximity to a warmer, more thoughtful, more empathic personality, but more surprisingly noticing that I actually quite enjoyed the change. I liked having a relationship that was less combative and less functional than I had been used to.

More strangely I noticed myself also softening philosophically, softening towards the notion of fate itself. I became more receptive to nebulous notions such as destiny, the thought that things might be 'meant to be'. Even, dare I admit it, open to the possibility of spiritual intervention.

Right now, however, in my current bereaved state, that notion of fate has changed from being a rather romantic, comforting thought into something more sinister. If I believe that our meeting was predestined, and right, then how can his death not also seem meant to be? And if so, why? What can that mean?

For many, many months in the wake of Bill's death my mind grappled with conundrums like this – was this all foretold? Was it somehow a punishment of me for something I had done? And if so, what was he, collateral damage? Was this some sort of karma and if so for which of us? What was I meant to learn from this? Why give him to me, show me a glimpse of happiness, then take him away? Round and round the spiral of unanswerable questions eddied my addled brain. No wonder I couldn't remember anything anyone ever said to me. I found myself questioning existence, faith, spirituality, the afterlife in a different way from ever before, relentlessly questioning and seeking non-existent answers. Why, how, who, what did this? And who am I without him? Such existential angst and a greater need to re-examine and redefine spirituality and belief is not uncommon after a bereavement, particularly a sudden one. But this spiralling down mental wormholes was unyielding, tying me up in such knots of confusion that I often wondered if I was going completely mad. I felt I was losing my grip on reality and sanity.

Rationally, of course, I knew grief came in many guises so maybe this was all part of it? Could anchoring myself in theoretical literature help me make sense of any of this?

~

Of the many theories about the grieving process, the most widely known is Elisabeth Kubler Ross's five stages, which she identified in 1969. This theory has so successfully found its way into common parlance that many grieving people take it as gospel, worrying there is something wrong with them if they don't experience each stage, or if they can't ever get to acceptance.

Fewer people know about William Worden's grief theory, in which he lists the four 'tasks' you must complete to get through grief. There are other, even less widely known theories too. But not many of these seem to address what I was currently experiencing – madness. Perhaps it's a bit too woolly and judgemental for the academic therapeutic world. Yet initially that is what I was feeling – a deep sense of unsettling madness. I thought I was losing my mind. And if I consult fictional literature I'm not alone – just look at Hamlet and Ophelia. Or Demi Moore in *Ghost*.

This all got me thinking. If something I was feeling so strongly wasn't talked about in our training, or in most academic literature, and if I was simultaneously being told I should be feeling things that I wasn't, then clearly these famous five stages, or the slightly less famous four tasks, aren't telling the full story. Yet there must be something in them or they wouldn't still be getting quoted so often. It seemed there were many layers hidden within the inadequate, catch-all label 'grief' that were worth exploring further – that needed to be explored further – for my own sanity if nothing else.

As I go through my own messy process, experience my own version of grief, I want to show you there are a myriad of routes through that madness, different lenses through which to experience grief, and varied languages with which we can try to make sense of the chaos into which we've been plunged. A chaos that, among other things, is very hard to convey in mere words. Could we find new ways of communicating – to ourselves and to others – how this unfamiliar, overwhelming and constantly changing maelstrom of emotional and practical upheaval really feels?

I will explore, from down here on the ground, hands muddied by my own frantic scrabblings for sense, what from among the many grief theories resonates for me, and what doesn't. I hope to demonstrate to you that your own grief will be fiercely individual. Yes, there are commonalities, and it can be hugely helpful to know that you are not alone, or going mad (at least not permanently), but there are also many ways in which you will not fit any sort of norm. That in itself is normal. Each of us brings our own personality, background and context to our grief – which is why it is also helpful to understand a little about what might have led to us responding as uniquely as we do. This is why, alongside exploring the various grief theories and trying them on for size, I also plan to draw on what I have learned from my broader psychotherapeutic training.

In psychotherapy we examine what makes us tick, question why our relationships and dynamics work as they do, and we aim for a greater level of insight and self-knowledge, a knowledge that might help us navigate the difficult moments in our lives – into which category the death of a loved one certainly falls. As with the grief theories, there are many different psychotherapeutic theories as to how to go about doing this. You have probably heard of the more well-known approaches – psychoanalytic, humanistic, existential, transpersonal, and so on. As an integrative psychotherapist I have studied many of these schools of thought, and plan to look at what each might offer to me – and maybe to you – in this time of grief.

The main point, however, is that there is no right or wrong way to do grief. It is always painful though, and long-lasting, and you cannot emerge unscathed or unchanged.

Down on the ground – or rather back in the hospital – I am to find this out myself, all too soon.

*   *   *

I walk away from my final goodbye to Bill, see my mother walking down the corridor towards me, and immediately burst into tears. It is becoming apparent that sympathy and a friendly face undo me, unlocking the emotion bubbling under the surface. Mum takes me home, offers to stay, and we pass a disjointed evening, during which we make a quick and reassuring return visit to the hospital later on to see the surgeon as he comes out of theatre. He tells us the surgery went well, and that Bill seems not to have suffered from any of the side effects that often accompany an aortic dissection, such as stroke or brain damage.

Somehow it is still only Sunday, and only a few hours have passed since Bill and I were happily making our plans to go out for a walk and lunch. Now Mum and I head back home in a very different emotional state. We are relieved by the surgeon's positive prognosis, but clearly not relieved enough to manage to sleep. The long dark hours of the night crawl by, at odds with my uncontrollably racing brain, which is intent on replaying every horrific moment of the day just gone, projecting images I'd rather not see onto the insides of my eyelids in vivid technicolour.

~

Eventually the dawn light of Monday brings the torturous night to an end. Mum goes back to her own house, and I go back to the hospital. I head up there on my bicycle this time, so convinced am I that all will be fine, that I will be chatting to Bill within minutes, and that normal life is about to resume.

On arrival I am told they have already tried to bring him round but that only the right-hand side of his body responded.

The left was paralysed, indicating that he had suffered a stroke in the night. They had immediately put him back under sedation again in order to monitor his brain activity and to avoid stressing him out while they work out what's going on.

I adapt to this new bit of information with shock and fear, but still with relative equanimity. Okay, so that's manageable, I tell myself. Lots of people have strokes. They require a bit of rehabilitation but that's all right, he'll just need a bit longer off work. Oh God, he's going to be a nightmare, he's so bloody impatient, and hates being housebound, he's going to be in a bad mood for weeks. Our forthcoming Paris weekend is definitely off, I realise, and I wonder if he will be okay for the big holiday booked in St Lucia next month. Practicalities are still uppermost in my mind as I cling to the familiar and reassuring feeling of having some sort of control, and cleave to an old confidence that life can continue relatively normally after this little hiatus.

I sit at the side of Bill's bed and talk to him, because the prevailing thinking is that he should still be able to hear me even though he is unconscious. He is wired up to what feels like a hundred machines while nurses come and go with clipboards and other medical paraphernalia. There is a lot of huddled whispering and a worried air about them all that I choose to ignore. If I believe it is all going to be all right, it will be. It can't not be. That is not an option. Amazing how convincing denial can be – I can't imagine it, so it can't happen. Not. An. Option. I witter on to him about who I have rung, what nice messages people have been sending back.

'I hope they wake you up soon Billy, it's really hard carrying on a one-sided conversation, you know. I'm running out of things to talk about. I need to hear your half of all this in order to have something to bounce off. I'm no good at chatting alone.'

Drying up, I decide to read to him. Another current theory is that people don't necessarily know what you are saying, they are just soothed by the sound of your familiar voice.

At regular intervals I stop reading and ask variously 'What are we waiting for?', 'What happens now?', 'When will you bring him round?'

I get very few straight answers. People are looking more and more worried. A part of me is registering this, but another part is shutting down this understanding as quickly as it pops up – like that fairground game where you have to hit the moles with a hammer as they stick their heads above ground in different spots. I am protecting myself, fighting to keep my cool, my sanity, my life as I know it intact. If I believe hard enough that everything will be okay, then it will be. In psychotherapeutic terms this could be termed magical thinking, the impossible belief that our thoughts alone can shape reality.

By late afternoon they seem – in as much as I am able or prepared to take in – to be saying that a blood clot, unleashed when the aorta first split, has taken up residence near Bill's brain and is gradually starving it of oxygen. I hear the phrase 'more serious stroke'. I readjust my thinking again:

'Okay, so it might be more than just a few weeks' rehabilitation. He might not be impatient and grumpy, because he might not have the brain capacity to be either of those things. Or anything else. We might have to sell the house, buy one of those adapted bungalows. Our future is looking decidedly unlike the future I thought we were going to have. But it's okay, we'll just adapt – us and the house together. I'll have to take on more clients to make ends meet. Will that be enough? What will we do if it's not?'

I force myself to continue reading to my unconscious husband, until I am told to go home: they need more tests, they want me out of the way, they promise to ring me when they have more news.

I wobble back on my bike, now much shakier and regretting that foolhardy insouciance that had propelled me out of the house this morning, thinking all was fine and that I was about to see him come round from the anaesthetic. As yesterday, I am struck by how elastic time has become and how quickly one's life and outlook can go from jaunty optimism to too-awful-to-contemplate dread. What has it been since I cycled up here, carefree and hopeful? Four hours? Five? How can Bill's phenomenal brain have plummeted so far so quickly? How can my life and prospects have dropped like a stone along with it?

Back home I phone my friend Julia and again a friendly ear allows me to finally give voice to my fears. I acknowledge the previously unsayable, unthinkable prospect that he might not survive: 'He's all I've got,' I tell her. 'I can't lose him, I'd have nothing.'

A few years earlier Bill and I had had to accept the fact that we couldn't have children. A decade of trying and an unrelenting march towards my mid-forties, and we had had to finally accept our fate. We looked at each other as our latest IVF attempt proved unsuccessful: 'That's it then, just you and me now,' we were forced to acknowledge.

It was awful and heartbreaking but, after ten years and five IVFs, not altogether unsurprising. It wasn't as if we hadn't been discussing this as a possible outcome for a good eight or so of those years. Once you've had one or two IVF failures it is really hard to stay positive, no matter how many more 'last' chances you give it, 'just in case'.

But still the realisation that we really did have no one but ourselves to love and rely on for the rest of our lives was tough and frightening. Not for our relationship – we both had utter faith and conviction that that would remain rock solid no matter what – but it was frightening to think how vulnerable we now were, having no one but the other person as close family. We thanked God and each other that we did indeed have each other; that we had such a strong and happy relationship; that we got on so fantastically, loved each other's company and were confident in ourselves. But our 'lot' really was to be tied up in no one but ourselves now forevermore – a compact little family of just two, with no outside distractions or additions.

It's not as if we don't have extended family; we do, but we don't see much of them and I, in particular, don't really factor them in to my calculations. Bill is less isolated than me – he loves his three siblings, their partners, and his seven nieces and nephews – but although they all get on well and keep in contact, they live relatively far away and like us are very busy, meaning that our lives are quite separate.

And I have a mum who, as we've seen, is prepared to drop everything and come to the hospital when I need her, which I appreciate hugely, but we aren't emotionally very close, nor do we have a huge amount in common. She is generally not the first person I turn to in a crisis, as yesterday had already proved when I texted two friends before her. In fact, I had developed a massive privacy wall around telling her anything about me – a trait developed in childhood that I had never managed to dismantle. It had taken me about six months to tell her I was getting married, and we had never discussed my trying for a baby. I assumed that she assumed that we didn't want one, as I had never been very maternal, and I was happy to go along with her assumption. I thought she would be happier thinking we were childless by choice, as I knew it would sadden her to know that we were saddened by our unchangeable situation. My father, with whom I had had more of a mutually confiding relationship, died four years ago and I still miss and mourn him dreadfully, while my sister and I are not close and haven't even spoken in the last two years. My niece is similarly distant and although she has recently had a baby, my great-nephew Frankie, I have yet to meet him.

So when I say to my friend Julia that if I lose Bill I will be losing everything, I really mean it, and I am beyond terrified. Although we are both very independent, with lots of outside interests, fundamentally we spend the vast majority of our lives together. We socialise together, stay in and veg in front of the TV together, holiday together, get cross with the same people and things together, take pleasure in theatre, and books and cycling, and food, and humour together. I can't lose him. If I do I will be losing my entire reason for living.

Julia tells me there is no point thinking that way, that all is still to hope for. I am not so sure.

*   *   *

I ring the hospital every half-hour and am persistently told that there is no new information. They know his brain has been badly affected by the stray blood that escaped when his aorta was torn. It formed a clot, which is now starving his brain of the oxygen it needs to stay alive, but they can't assess how bad the damage is. They need Charing Cross's MRI again for that, but it is too dangerous to move him there from his current bed in Hammersmith's cardiology department because, so soon after heart surgery, his heart is too frail and needs constant monitoring.

Again, I am fighting not to scream at the cruelness of the austerity cuts that have led to the separation of these two specialties onto two different sites, miles apart. Again I try not to go there, try not to let myself believe Bill's situation could have been preventable, that had he had access to that MRI more quickly – both prior to surgery, and post – he might have survived. Two missed opportunities to save him. But thinking that is too painful, the thought that he could have been saved, that I cannot stand. It is actually easier to accept that it would have happened, no matter what, rather than dwell on the 'might have been'.

I sit at home chewing my nails, texting and phoning other friends and family. About 9 p.m. my mother turns up again to accompany me through our second night of waiting and not knowing. Time ticks on and still the hospital staff don't call back. We decide to try to get some sleep, but we stay fully clothed, primed to rush back to the hospital if necessary. Mum lies on the bed next to me, as the idea of being left alone, even with her just in the next room, is unbearable. We lie there beside each other, both wide awake, unable to sleep. I put on a meditation podcast to try to calm us. Still we don't sleep. We just remain there supine and immobile while an American Buddhist instructs us in deep breathing and muscle relaxation. We try to follow the instructions. We couldn't be more tense.

A couple of hours pass. The phone rings. Someone from the hospital tells me that Bill's condition is deteriorating. There is one more thing they can try, but they are not hopeful that it will work: they are going to take him back to Charing Cross, to the neurology department, and are going to saw a piece of his skull off to let the rising pressure out. They don't think it will do any good, but it's the only thing left to try. They are pretty sure he will not survive.

I allow the words to sit there in the air between my phone and my ear. I hang up. I tell my mother what they have said.

She tells me I must have misheard, they can't be saying it is all over. I am numb and in shock. I tell her that I don't really know what they said. Maybe I did get it wrong. I ask her to phone them back and get them to repeat to her what they have just told me as I must have misunderstood. She calls them back, asks them to tell her the situation as I haven't grasped it properly. They repeat to her what they told me. She hangs up. We look at each other. There are no words.

We go downstairs, get in the car, and she drives us to Charing Cross Hospital. It is the middle of the night. We see one of the nurses from Hammersmith standing outside having a smoke. He tells us they have just arrived, and that Bill has been taken upstairs. He directs us there. On arrival we are again shepherded into yet another waiting room. Fluorescent strips cast brutal light across this unwelcoming room and reveal a family, spread out across the plastic chairs, grey of face, half sitting, half lying, trying to sleep. They have clearly been there for days awaiting news of whoever it is they are in the process of losing. It is the saddest, bleakest sight I have ever seen, and I am to join their ranks.

Mum and I find some spare chairs and perch, still unable to speak. A doctor arrives and tells us that Bill's condition has deteriorated in the ambulance down here and it is not even worth attempting the operation they had mentioned. It will do no good.

There is nothing more they can do.

~

It takes three days for the last breaths to leave Bill's body.

Even though he is brain dead and there is no hope for recovery, nevertheless he cannot be officially declared dead until twelve specific conditions, as set out in law, are met. Bill still has some residual gases in his lungs, which means that he fails the twelfth test. For three days I sit in the misery of that hospital, waiting for this last bit of air to leave his lungs.

I feel like I am in an episode of BBC1's hospital soap opera, *Casualty*. This is doubly surreal because when he was still acting Bill twice appeared in the show. He used to tell funny stories about his small roles as Gordon in a 1993 episode, and Trevor in 1998. One of these characters, I forget which, was a philanderer whose wife and girlfriend both turn up at his bedside after an accident. Luckily, I don't have that particular scenario to contend with, but I do have to deal with the comings and goings of the close friends and members of his family who come to say goodbye, all with the same stricken, ashen look on their faces. No one is more devastated and shell-shocked than Bill's siblings Janey, James and Kate. It is only four months since their mother Georgine died – also unexpectedly – and we have spent much of the last four months getting together at her house, grieving her, reminiscing and trying to sort out her many, many effects. Bill led the eulogies at her funeral, and we have a ceremony to bury her ashes alongside her husband, their dad, booked for a week hence. Impossible to believe that now we must do the same for her son.

Hours become days and it all passes in a blur. At night I go home to sleep, or more accurately, to lie, not sleeping, on what I still think of as 'our' bed. During the day in the hospital I variously stand, sit or lie next to Bill in his bed or I cede the space to the others who come to visit him. I feel like the bad hostess of a weird and terrible cocktail party – greeting people, showing them to Bill's bedside, leaving them there to say their goodbyes, offering bad coffee and chocolate. And tissues.

I too feel like I am now an actor on *Casualty* or some other TV or film set. I've seen these same scenes so often on television shows and now I am part of the action. It must be a set, it can't be real, because another part of me is watching the actor me going through the motions that I've seen others do so many times on screen; playing the part of the grieving widow – greeting the visitors, talking gently to Billy, confusedly to doctors, now crying, now smiling as the next visitor arrives. I can see myself there doing these things, but I am also not there. I watch myself have moments of collapse, and moments of clarity. I experience hellish, lonely nights when I long for company, followed by busy, chaotic days filled with others when I long to be alone.

Most of the time I feel nothing. I am numb. I am not really there.

~

In therapy we call this phenomenon 'dissociation', that feeling of not really being present. Many people will relate to this for many reasons, not all of them to do with grief.

Dissociation is a natural response to trauma and comes about because the mind can only bear so much painful reality at a time. It is one of a series of responses that work to cushion us from severe pain. It means the organism is protecting itself, developing its own strategy to remove itself from danger and take metaphorical shelter somewhere safe. Shutting the door on the monster, so to speak.

Trauma happens when we fear for our lives or the lives of those closest to us. It can be the result of a one-off event – something like an earthquake, car crash, rape, losing a husband overnight; or it can result from long-term debilitating fear for one's survival – such as that experienced by refugees fleeing their homes, soldiers or civilians stuck in war zones, even children living with caretakers who abuse them. To a child with no means of escape from a frightening home environment, that is just as much a survival issue as for a soldier trapped in a war, or an imprisoned kidnap victim.

When survival is at stake and the resulting terror is too much for our thinking brains to process – our instincts take over. This is not a conscious choice, but a primeval, hard-wired, physiological response, an instinctive reaction that has remained the same over millennia. Despite millions of years of evolution, when survival is threatened our old, hard-wired responses still kick in powerfully.

In evolutionary terms that's a good thing – it means we leap out of the way of a snake or a speeding car, before our brains have even worked out what is happening. It can therefore be a life-saving function.

This unstoppable physiological response is better known as the fight/flight/freeze response. It happens at a non-conscious, automatic and involuntary level and is useful and necessary – it's adaptive, our bodies saving the day. To understand why and how it works to save us we need to go way back – to have a brief look at the early days of our evolution.

The earliest version of our brain only had a primitive, basic body to keep alive. It controlled heart rate, breathing and balance, and that was just about it. We were simple creatures then. This early, uncomplicated brain is still with us. It is called our reptilian brain, as a nod to the state we were in when it first developed.

As we evolved into more complex beings, a larger, correspondingly more complex brain evolved around this reptilian brain. The newer, more responsible 'limbic' brain came into being to manage our increasingly sophisticated needs. It took up the reins as control panel for our emotions, unconscious responses and, most importantly, our survival instinct.

Later still our needs and sophistication expanded yet further, causing the third part of the brain, the neocortex, to grow around the two older parts. This newest addition is responsible for language, abstract thought, rationality, consciousness and the processing that can manage and interpret experience and contribute to a healthy sense of self.

When we experience trauma, when our very survival feels at stake, just when you would think we would need our most evolved brain the most, it goes offline, concedes power to the older, less evolved limbic brain. Why?

Well, primarily because it is at those moments that we need action rather than thought. The limbic system, dating back as it does to a far-off time when our bodies were more central to our lifestyles than they are in our current static, technologically motivated world, is more intimately connected to our autonomic nervous system and thus to our bodies and instincts. This makes it more reactive and quicker than the neocortex, whose sophistication of cognitive thought has slowed it down.

Our autonomic nervous system has two complementary halves: the sympathetic half, which promotes our get-up-and-go instinct – the internal caffeine supply, if you like – and the parasympathetic half, which promotes the rest-and-digest instinct – an internal chill pill, we can call it. It is regulated by the hypothalamus, which affects our arousal in response to emotional events. Within the hypothalamus lies the amygdala, the body's smoke detector. When it senses an emergency situation it sounds an alarm that primes the body to respond to the crisis by producing stress hormones such as cortisol and adrenaline. These race the danger message around the body, causing it to react instinctively, fire up the sympathetic nervous system to full throttle and leap into survival mode. This also means shutting down all non-essential functions to keep the heart pumping, the lungs breathing, the legs and arms surging with blood – the whole body primed, poised and ready to act.

This is the limbic brain doing what it does best, marshalling the troops for action. What it doesn't need is the slower, more logical, rational brain, the neocortex, getting in its way with all that annoying, time-wasting thinking it does. So in that moment of trauma the two brains stop communicating and each goes off into its own silo. The limbic brain, like Jack Bauer pulling his earpiece out so he doesn't have to listen to Mission Control trying to run the show, just gets on with doing what needs doing on the ground. (If this reference doesn't work for you, just pick whichever action-hero-going-rogue you most identify with, and you'll get the general gist.)

So, while the stress hormones and survival responses unleashed by the limbic brain are in action, the neocortex is unable to reopen the lines of communication. At this point we are in full fight/flight/freeze mode.

While in this moment of limbic, bodily response we are poised and ready to use all that adrenaline to either fight the enemy with our new-found superhuman strength or, if the enemy is too enormous, to instead use it to flee for our lives. Both fight and flight provoke hyper-arousal in our system, arousal we can put to good use to try to save ourselves. It is really helpful.

Except sometimes the situation is so hopeless that we can neither fight nor flee. Sometimes the enemy is too all-powerful. But, just like a wounded deer that has neither the vigour to run nor the strength to fight the lion, there is one more powerful resource we can call on. This resource, the third weapon in the limbic brain's arsenal, is the freeze response – playing dead. Limp and barely breathing, the seemingly dead deer makes for a far less appetising meal to its aggressor, like something in the supermarket being beyond its sell-by date. And even if the lion is hungry enough to overlook the possible repercussions and chow down anyway, this playing dead, this shutting down of practically all visible physical responses, has another advantage – internally it creates a natural anaesthetic, meaning that the deer will feel less pain as the jaws inevitably sink into its neck.

We humans, when under threat, go into our version of this frozen 'rabbit in headlights' state where we literally cannot move. Instead we do what we <u>are</u> still able to do, which is to move our attention. For instance, we dissociate, we float away, we focus on something outside ourselves like the wallpaper or a shoe; anything to pretend we are not really there and to shut down the messages of pain coming from the body.

Such an instantaneous, dramatic response comes at a price, however. When we are being prepared by our body to fight or flee, the adrenal system mobilises the activating sympathetic nervous system, increasing the heartbeat and deepening breathing, causing hyper-arousal of the system. Pressing its foot on the accelerator, so to speak.

And switching tactics and initiating the freeze response requires a rapid and sudden shift into dominance by the parasympathetic nervous system to slow the heartbeat and the breath – like slamming on the brakes in an emergency stop.

Pulling out all the stops in this way takes a massive toll on your body – you are basically doing the equivalent of pressing both accelerator and brake at the same time. The freeze response is therefore a last resort, only called upon when the situation is truly hopeless, when things are even more dangerous than those times where fight or flight might still have had a chance of success.

The numbing effects of shock and the distancing effects of dissociation are both part of the freeze response, also known as hypo-arousal. It may save your life, but there is a downside. Less breath means less oxygen in the blood, which means less energy and less brainpower, and you may move and function in a rather slow and spacey way, or just seem completely absent or unaware of what is going on.

So, feeling numb and dissociated for most of those early days was actually my limbic brain harnessing my nervous system to protect me from the horrors of reality. A reality that, if fully taken on board, would have been too much to bear. Bill, my closest, my only family, not to mention my best friend, was abandoning me. If my response were allowed to go unmediated, it would feel as if my ongoing survival was at stake. So freezing stepped in to save me.

Looking back more objectively at myself in the hospital, I can see that I was shut down in freeze mode most of the time. And my bodily functions were responding and shutting down too, which is all part of this response.

'I'm going to the loo,' I tell Bill. 'Yes, AGAIN,' in answer to the unspoken question that I know he is thinking. Or would be, if he could still think.

I run to the loo every few minutes. When I get there it's always rather horrifying to find how my bowels have turned to water. And, even though I can't eat and am on the verge of throwing up the whole time (although I am not actually sick), my body seems to be straining to evacuate as much as it can via that route as well as down below. I feel completely drained, literally and metaphorically – fight/flight/freeze is naturally shutting down all extraneous functions not directly related to survival.

I also haven't slept in days and seem to have lost my memory, possibly even my whole brain. I forget large chunks of information given to me by the doctors and the organ donation staff – euphemistically referred to as 'specialist nurses' – and ask for everything to be repeated. People do of course repeat everything for me, over and over again. Everyone is incredibly kind, gentle and solicitous.

I spend about 90 per cent of my time in this numb, dissociated state, but at times reality does break through. When it does, I feel like my insides are being ripped out through my mouth. I sob and shake uncontrollably. Sometimes these breakdowns occur when I am with friends, who have to hold me till it subsides. Sometimes they happen while I am lying alongside Billy in his hospital bed, the shakes contained by the fact that I am sandwiched uncomfortably between the safety bars of the bed on one side, and his immobile body on the other. My tears drench the thin hospital sheet covering him, but his own lifeless skin below is no longer able to feel how sodden I am making him.

Meltdowns aside, these are normally the calmest and most peaceful moments, just Billy and me alone together, not having to worry about other people, oblivious to what is going on around us. Despite being uncomfortably squished up alongside each other, my head on his chest, feeling it lift and fall and blanking out the knowledge that it is only doing so thanks to a machine, this position nevertheless feels familiar, us lying together and chatting. Well, obviously it is only me doing the chatting, but he still feels present somehow despite his silence. As I talk I recount memories, tell him how much I love him and will miss him, but I also try to reassure him that it is okay for him to go now, that I will manage, that all my friends, and his, will be there for me.

Then we reach the worst moment of all, and it takes me by surprise. This is terrifying, can't-speak-can't-breathe-think-I-am-dying-want-to-be-dying meltdown. It is the first time this has happened to me with such all-consuming power, but sadly it won't be the last. It happens at the end of the third day of waiting for Bill to pass – or should that be fail – his twelfth test and be declared officially dead.

I have been sent back to the waiting room while the doctor carries out the tests once more. She comes to find me and tells me that it is finally over. It is late afternoon on Thursday the ninth of November.

The doctor is kind. 'How are you?' she asks with a worried look.

'I am relieved,' I tell her, which is clearly not the answer she was expecting. But I have known he was dead in all but name since Monday night and these three days in hospital have been horrific and strange and peaceful and lonely and terrifying all at once. Because of the twelfth test hold-up I have been told maybe ten or so times over the course of these three days that his death is imminent, and that I should go and say my final goodbye.

Having now repeated this heart-rending scene of hugging him, sobbing, saying goodbye and telling him how much I love him ten times or more, only to be told again and again that it was a false alarm, he's still not officially dead and I will have to do it all again in an hour, I feel worn out and in despair. There really are only so many takes of this horror film that I can manage. It feels unbearably cruel to have to keep replaying it. So, the knowledge that he is finally gone actually feels like an end to a long-drawn-out torture for both of us: he is released, hopefully to rest in peace, and I can leave the hospital.

So, I don't cry, I admit my relief, and the doctor clearly thinks I haven't understood. But I have. Or I think I have. Until, that is, the organ donation staff step in to tell me that they will now be taking him to surgery to have his organs removed. And suddenly I collapse. Out of nowhere. The thought of my beloved, fragile, vulnerable Billy being taken to have an operation without me there to hold him and see him through it feels unbearable. I feel a desperate need to protect him. He cannot feel anything, hasn't felt anything since Monday, and yet I am suddenly like a lioness protecting her cub and can't bear to have this happen to him. Please be nice to him, I sob to the organ donation nurses, don't leave him on his own, hold his hand to the end. They promise me they will stay with him. It feels desperately important for him not to be by himself. I have no idea why, but I can't stand the idea that he might be taking this final journey alone.

And I too now have to face how alone I am. Our tiny family of two has just lost half its number, leaving me exposed and vulnerable. The momentary relief I felt when the hospital part of the ordeal was over is now replaced with the prospect of a different and far more long-lasting type of ordeal. How do I continue without him? Life as I knew it has imploded. A bomb has detonated, blowing to smithereens the supposedly safe ship in which I'd obliviously been sailing along, unsuspectingly secure in what I thought was its robustness and seaworthiness. Now all that remains are shards of wood, currently raining down and spearing me as I flail around helplessly in the middle of a stormy dark ocean.

I had wanted to leave the hospital, but now that I can, where am I to go? Am I really meant to go home? Does home exist without Bill in it? Or am I returning simply to four walls and a roof, a shell with no heart, as I too am now just a collection of skin and bone holding together an empty void within?

What am I without him? I am nothing, and I have nothing, and I do not want to live.

That I do is entirely down to an amazing group of friends. During those three days in hospital they had not only pulled out all the stops to be there at my side, but they had also organised a 'babysitting' rota for me on my return home, because they and I knew that I shouldn't be left alone. We were all afraid of what might happen if I was.

~

The fear for my safety was instinctive, but in fact its validity can also be proved by research. Statistically, we were right to be worried. Not only might I follow through on an emerging and growing desire to kill myself, but no matter what decision my brain reached, my body could have even decided to take matters into its own hands.

When looked at scientifically, it seems that it is actually possible to die of a broken heart. Recent studies have come up with some surprising facts: widows and widowers are at a 41 per cent higher risk of dying in the three months following their spouse's death.

Their bodies reveal they have higher levels of inflammation in the bloodstream, and lower heart-rate variability, which is an indicator of heart health. Both these factors increase the risk of cardiac problems and can lead to premature death. The study also showed 20 per cent higher levels of the symptoms of depression, while another study found that widows and widowers were more likely to have a heart attack or stroke within thirty days of the death of their spouse. This can be explained by the fact that severe emotional stress affects the nervous system, as we have already seen with the fight/flight/ freeze response.

Although frightening and concerning for the spouses among us, this is actually the sort of statistic that I love – a study born of scientifically rigorous research that basically confirms what we all instinctively know, and which poems, songs, music, literature and art have been telling us for years – our hearts really can break when we lose the one we love.

It also bolsters the, to me, self-evident notion that body and mind work as a holistic system and that our bodies manifest our emotional states very literally. Grief affects us physically – externally in the aching joints, tiredness, backache, susceptibility to illness and other horrible ailments, and also internally at the very deep level of our crucial organs, even down at a cellular, hormonal and respiratory level.

My body is certainly feeling the effects of the shock, alternating numb invisibility with all too discernible aching. It feels incapable of normal – has no idea what on earth normal even is now – functioning. I no longer know how to eat or sleep or wash or dress myself. I've worn the same clothes for five days. Parts of my brain are in overdrive, but the corporeal me is in some sort of parallel universe. The 'babysitting' rota drawn up by my friends kicks in. It has fallen to my friend Julia to get me home and to spend the first night and the next day with me. We trained as psychotherapists together, but in her former career she was a probate lawyer. If I wanted to define the perfect person to have with me in this situation it would be someone who has both the therapeutic skills to cope with a shocked, grieving widow and the legal and practical skills to help get the awful admin under way – and who just happens to be one of my best friends. It is uncanny how well she fits the bill. She's straight out of Central Casting in fact.

The list of things that have to be done after a death is endless. First job – find Bill's will. This I do relatively easily, but it doesn't take Julia's legal eagle eye long to spot that he hasn't signed it. I can still choose to carry out his wishes as per the will (and I will), but legally he has died intestate, which means there will be even more paperwork involved in administering it. It's going to be complicated, as there is also the question of Bill's business to sort out, so we visit two sets of law firms to decide whom to ask to represent me. We choose the second, having very inappropriately got the giggles at how bad the first one had been at knowing how to 'deal' with me. I wasn't even crying, was relatively together in my queries, yet he directed all his answers straight to Julia, referring to me constantly as 'she', even though I was sitting right in front of him. I felt like I was trapped in an Alan Partridge sketch, but I actually started to feel grateful to him for his lack of 'bedside manner'; it showed me that even in the midst of this torment, I still had a sense of humour and could enjoy the absurdity of the situations I was finding myself in. And I had the added glow of warmth that came from knowing how much Bill would have enjoyed the comedy of it.

Another major task is to inform my clients that I will not be available for a while. Back in that now impossible-to-believe-it-ever-existed world, a world where I thought Bill would be emerging unscathed from his operation, I had cancelled them all just for the following week. It is now clear I will be in no fit state to see them for far longer than that. Two of my therapist friends divide my client list between them and offer each person help in finding another therapist to take my place. All my clients turn down this option and say they will wait for me. They send me their love. Their concern for me breaks my heart further – it's not meant to be them worried about me.

Day two and it is my friend Sherie's turn to babysit me. We ring and visit funeral homes and funeral venues, speak to humanist celebrants, start to choose music. Bill's invalid, but nevertheless helpful, will specified that he did not want a church funeral, so we look for other options. We then start phoning round banks and the myriad other official places that need to be notified of his death, and cancelling things like phone contracts, gym membership, credit cards, magazine subscriptions, and more. How ridiculously complicated our lives are nowadays. How many passwords we have. Thank goodness Bill loved a good list.

Day three, my cousin Jonathan comes to look over Bill's financial affairs with me and then helps me back to the hospital to get the cause-of-death paperwork. There he hands me over to another cousin, Anya, who leads a now very drained and droopy me to the Register Office at Hammersmith Town Hall, where they will issue a formal death certificate.

Throughout all this I realise that it is hard to predict which are the things that are likely to set me off. I had again got the giggles while Jonathan and I were in the hospital awaiting the paperwork and we heard a request for a paramedic to make their way urgently to the morgue. 'Isn't it a bit late for that?' we whispered to each other.

But come the moment in the Register Office, laughter of any kind is in very short supply. It doesn't help of course that the waiting room brings Anya and me into close proximity with those there to register births and marriages – how dare these people be happy and getting on with their lives? It gets worse once we are ushered into a characterless, claustrophobic, box-like administration office. I soon start to unravel. I make it through his name, address, occupation, and all the other questions fired at me by the registrar as she types the information into the computer she is hiding behind. But the request for Bill's date of birth undoes me. My voice cracks and the tears fall as I try to say 'Seventeenth of April 1961'. This date has been hugely important to me to know and to celebrate for the last fourteen years, and from this date on it will no longer have any relevance. It will not matter. No one will ever again ask for his date of birth. This somehow symbolises his 'gone-ness'. Now all I will ever be asked for, the only thing now important, will be his date of death. And that is never going to be cause for celebration. I weep quietly and feel sorry for Anya being the one to be lumbered with me at this particular low point, when I can no longer even muster the energy to pretend to be doing okay. She, on the other hand, does a very good job of seeming not to mind, and when we finally make it home she gives me the present she's bought me. I change into these fluffy, sparkly pyjamas and wait patiently for the dinner she is in the process of cooking. I feel like a five-year-old being prepared for bed. It is not an unwelcome feeling.

On day four Mariana arrives, day five Inge turns up, and so the days churn by. Tasks get slowly ticked off the list, loving friends come and go, scheduled by a rota determined by the WhatsApp group they have created. These are friends from all different walks of life, and many have never met each other, yet they come together in the group and work out how to provide seamless care and support. I float through in a daze, realising I have no choice but to go with whatever emerges – to try to ride out the small, manageable waves of clarity and productivity, but also to accept being thwacked by the tidal waves of grief, which come, as waves do, rhythmically and relentlessly, pounding the shore of my sanity, leaving me collapsed and helpless in the face of their power. Some I can weather, while others tumble me beneath their strength to the point where I fear I will never again find which way is up and be able to take in air rather than water.

In among it all I am amazed that I can still find humour, but I also know Bill would want me to do so. Comedy ran through his veins. I even start to wonder if he is possibly orchestrating some of it. One of the many tasks I find myself embroiled in is the daily checking of his emails, messages, Facebook, WhatsApp groups and other paraphernalia of modern life, in case anything important comes in or there's anyone still to be told. As a Green Party member and former election candidate, Bill is on the local Green Party WhatsApp group. Obviously, the other members do not realise that I am now monitoring what they are posting. They start a thread about Bill's death: 'Have you heard about Bill Cashmore?', 'He was a nice guy', 'What a shame', 'Does anyone know what happened?', and so on, mainly unsurprising, innocuous stuff. But then they get practical:

'What's the protocol in these situations?'

'Should we send a representative to the funeral?'

'Is anyone available to go?'

'Should we send the widow something?'

My friends and I spend many happy moments composing a reply to this last one, coming up with something along the lines of:

'The widow is particularly fond of roses, orchids, Prestat salted caramel truffles, Hummingbird cupcakes and Aspinall's stationery.'

They send flowers.

I visit the solicitors who Julia and I have decided to engage. This time I am in a worse state and can't stop crying. One of the solicitors – male, old – urges the other solicitor – male, young – to go and find me some tissues. He comes back many, many minutes later and, avoiding my eye, and any conversation, shoves a wodge of kitchen roll at me. Luckily this too now makes me laugh. Probate lawyers are surprisingly ill-equipped to deal with a bereaved woman, despite this presumably being a bit of an occupational hazard. Or maybe other bereaved people just hold it in better than I do? Still, it was all worth it because Bill would have adored the kitchen roll moment, and the look of sheer terror on the young solicitor's face as he realised he had to interact with me in that state. Bill would probably even have written these scenes into one of his plays. Because yes, as well as being an actor and businessman Bill also wrote plays, as well as newspaper articles and his own one-man shows, which he loved performing. Bill was a man who liked to keep busy and pack things in.

As do I. And as I continue to do, despite the weirdness and unfamiliarity of my new unwelcome universe. The days pass, and I even manage to enjoy the more ludicrous and surreal moments like this. But I also occasionally collapse. Most of the time, however, I float through in a dissociated haze, getting on with all the necessary and unending practical tasks that now assail me. I even manage to deal with them relatively effectively.

~

How do I remain efficient and functioning in the face of this unimaginable horror? It is of course partly the numbing, freezing effects of the shock and trauma, but it is also partly that in times of crisis we revert to type. We resort to ways of being that have protected us historically and we call on whatever behaviours have saved us in the past.

We all operate on two interconnected levels simultaneously. Our thinking brain works at an intellectual, cognitive level, helping us reason our way through a problem logically and analytically. And at the same time, on a more embodied, emotional level, our feelings, moods, energy levels are also reacting, letting us know how we feel about something, what our gut instinct is.

Sometimes those two things are in sync. For example, we may cognitively 'think' we need to take it easy and not push ourselves when we're not feeling strong, and simultaneously we 'feel' the same – our bodies are sending us the equivalent message that we are tired, sad, don't feel up to facing the world. All well and good – we know what feels right for the moment, and our brains see the logic and are on board with that. So we relax, we cancel plans, we stay in, eat something nourishing and have an early night.

But at other times brain and body are out of sync. Those sad, drained feelings of needing to hibernate and hunker down are there, but our brains are perhaps telling us instead that it's not healthy to stay in and 'mope', or that we should be 'over it', that people will expect us to be back at work by now, or whatever it is that is our own habitual mantra as to why we ought to keep going. Our thinking minds are trying to override the feelings, forcing us to go against our emotional state, so that what was initially a single issue – I'm drained and need a break – becomes a multilayered issue, adding ambivalence and conflict and often guilt into the mix as well: 'I'm bad for feeling this, I'm lazy, I need to force myself to do what I think is right', or some such equivalent (and no doubt familiar) mantra. Suddenly all is not so harmonious, and an internal battle rages, draining our already limited amount of energy still further.

This is just one tiny example of the myriad negotiations and compromises that our feeling selves have with our cognitive selves every minute of every day, and not just when grieving. Most of the time this is not at a conscious level, but is going on subconsciously, out of awareness, and we have no idea why we feel so disjointed or discombobulated or dissatisfied: all those 'dis' words that suggest discord between our minds and bodies. When the two are in sync, internal peace reigns, but when they are not then that disharmony brings a whole raft of other issues in its wake. Depending on the current situation, and our response to that, the mind can either help or hinder our emotional world. The opposite is also true – the emotions can prove sometimes useful, sometimes overwhelming and unhelpful to the thinking mind.

But to be aware of this first requires an acceptance of mind/body unity – which is basically a therapist's way of saying that the mind and body are part of a holistic system and work together. This is in contrast to an approach that reigned supreme for many years. The seventeenth-century philosopher René Descartes famously proclaimed: 'I think therefore I am', which led to us all, for many centuries, believing that the mind and the body worked separately, causing medical doctors and mental health therapists to believe they were each working on different systems. Nowadays very few therapists, and not many doctors, believe this Cartesian dualism.

I describe myself, as, among other things, an integrative, embodied, relational psychotherapist, which means that I believe very strongly that we cannot separate body and mind, because they interact constantly – sometimes happily, sometimes less so. One of the aims of therapy is to allow them equal weight and give them equal attention in order to promote balance. The hope is that by giving clients the chance to discuss various situations from their past and their present, and those they imagine happening in the future, together we can start to understand when and how body and mind work in harmony, and conversely when and how they are at odds and fighting. We can start to see when one half is dominating while the other half is not getting enough of a look-in, and therefore think about when it is appropriate to allow each to take control in the moment.

~

Therapists sometimes jokingly resort to a very reductionist way of categorising people into two types: those who 'feel but can't deal', and those who 'deal but can't feel'.

If you are a dealer rather than a feeler, when crises hit you will go straight up into your head and into coping mode. You will shut down any connection with your body and emotions in favour of putting your brain into overdrive: setting it to work organising, planning, solving, thinking through all the logical and rational ways to deal with whatever is going on, keeping alive the illusion that you can control the situation. This is also referred to as a top-down solution – the brain sends the command downwards to the body, telling it how to behave. I am, by nature, a dealer. This brings both advantages and disadvantages. On the plus side, this mode of being prevents me from having to acknowledge my instinctive terror; it also doesn't allow me to feel the anguish and help-lessness of my lack of control. My mind tries to 'rise above' the pain, fear, sadness, anger, or any of those other annoying emotions that threaten to overwhelm me if I give them an inch of room in which to make themselves felt.

Many of us practise this cutting-off technique and most of us are completely unaware that we are doing it, so ingrained is that way of being. It is one of the reasons why we therapists are endlessly – and very annoyingly to some of our clients – saying: 'Get in touch with the feeling, stay with the feeling.'

Back in my twenties, when my first therapist used to ask what I was feeling, I was completely floored by the question. I would say, 'I think that what I feel is . . .'

She would patiently explain that thinking about what I was feeling was not the same as actually feeling it. But I had no idea what she meant and would concentrate harder on trying to 'work out' – brain into action again – what she could possibly want me to say. I was cut off from the neck down and no information from my body could get through, so used was I to thinking my way out of situations. Little did I understand then that this habit of being stuck in my head was one of the many things that led me into therapy in the first place. I thought I wasn't dealing well enough, could never have countenanced the thought that actually I was dealing too well – to the exclusion of all else.

There are advantages and disadvantages to being a 'dealer'. On the plus side, we look like we are in charge, we get things done, we appear to be coping and making good decisions. The downside is that this exacts a heavy price. There is always a trade-off. By creating what is in effect a sort of internal Cartesian dualism (I think therefore I am) and steamrollering our emotions out of the picture, we are also cutting ourselves off from the very useful information that our bodies and emotions could be giving us, providing a more 360-degree way of understanding ourselves.

More importantly, this strategy doesn't work in the long term because feelings can never be obliterated just by force of mind over matter. They will always come back to bite us. They can be temporarily squashed down out of sight, sometimes for years, but that is all they are – just hidden for the time being. They still exist and still need to be attended to at some point. And if they are not, they will find other ways to seep out, often in ways that we have even less control over – maybe in uncontrolled outbursts at inappropriate times, maybe in illnesses or depression, maybe in a breakdown many years later. You can run but you can't hide – at some point you need to listen, or those feelings will MAKE you listen.

After many months in therapy, I learned first to understand the question – to realise that thinking about what I feel is not the same as actually feeling it. Then, later, after many *years* in therapy, I learned how to tune in and recognise those feelings. Later still I became able to allow them expression without overwhelm, fear or judgement. However, in times of crisis – and I would definitely term what I was going through in the wake of Bill's death a crisis – old habits die hard and, like most of us, I reverted to old ways of being; ways of coping that had protected me in the past when faced with terror. In short, for much of the time in the hospital and immediately after, I regressed, returning to the behaviours that feel most familiar to me.

But what of the other type of person – the 'feelers'? Before I go there, remember that there is no judgement involved in any of this – we are all just getting by in whatever way has, historically, proved to be the most effective way for us, depending on our upbringing, temperament and experiences. Even more importantly, these distinctions are not rigid, comprehensive or permanent. They are not life sentences, a declaration of 'who you are' forevermore. They are just one of many ways of viewing certain traits. So, some of us may tend more towards one way of being in certain situations – say at work – but towards the other in different situations – say within relationships. Or it might be that when feeling on top of things we tend towards one way and when feeling more stressed, we tend to the other. They are fluid and changeable and do not define you. But having a sense of which way you tend to lean, and when, can be useful.

So how do feelers engage with a crisis? They pretty much do what it says on the tin – they feel their way through it, they really let it all out.

If you are a feeler you respond instinctively to your feelings. You are very much in touch with the emotional information being signalled by your body. This is also called 'bottom-up' processing – feelings express themselves without being filtered through the mind's 'do I need to modify my responses?' function. Here they run the show, shouting so loudly that the brain can't get a word in.

For instance, you may see someone being bullied or attacked and, without a thought for your own safety, instinctively rush to help. You may stub your toe and immediately scream in pain despite the fact that you are in a posh restaurant and all the other diners are looking at you in horror. You may see your partner talking to another person and immediately start raging that they are being unfaithful.

When Bill first clutched his chest in pain a feeler might have started screaming, burst into tears, immediately rung an ambulance, then been too overwrought to remember their address. Or they might have been so worked up that they needed help getting into the ambulance because their legs had also given out due to the sheer terror of not knowing what was going on. They probably would not have calmly texted a couple of people an understated query about how busy they were – as I the dealer did; instead they would likely have rung everyone they knew and begged them to tell them what to do. In short, it might have felt like their world was caving in and they were helpless, only able to cry and panic and reach out to others for help.

Such a state is often called flooding – when feelings are so overwhelming that our brains are deluged and cannot function in the face of so much emotion but instead go 'offline' as though in fight/flight/freeze mode.

Bill was more of a feeler – I have already written about the screams of anguish he would emit when in pain, or enraged, or scared. His brain couldn't help him modify his responses because in those moments he was all feeling and the mind couldn't get a look in.

As with dealers, there are advantages and disadvantages to this way of being. Sometimes it can be helpful, sometimes not so much. One advantage is that you know what you are feeling, you don't have to think about it, you are in touch with a sensitive side. This can often mean you are warmer and more sympathetic to friends who are in need of comfort. The dealers among us are more likely to offer practical solutions to help solve an issue, whereas the feeler will understand that what is really needed is a hug and some sympathetic noises.

It also means that you keep the lines of communication open to painful feelings and thus can more easily get in touch with the pleasurable ones too. You can feel joy and happiness spontaneously and instinctively without the brain's filter wondering if you 'ought' to be okay with whatever is happening. Another advantage can be that, by getting the emotions out and over with quickly, they don't sit and fester and reveal themselves in more insidious ways like resentment or delayed explosions.

Because Bill and I were at opposite ends of the spectrum when it came to feeling and dealing, our arguments in the early days of our relationship could quickly become very unbalanced. He was quick to anger – would shout his displeasure very loudly – but was also very quick to recover; within minutes it would have dissipated, and he would apologise. I, on the other hand, being a dealer, was slow to recognise my anger and slow to recover. I let things that annoyed me go on for far too long, my brain not really registering the growing irritation, or maybe noticing it but telling me to get over it, only for it to explode many months later over the tiniest of things, causing me to sulk for days.

I hated what I saw as Bill's lack of control and impetuousness, whereas he hated the fact that I couldn't just recognise what I needed to say, say it and move on. Obviously over the years, as we got to learn this about ourselves and each other, we became better able to temper our natural tendencies in the interest of marital harmony and understanding the other's point of view, and thus both come to operate from a more balanced position.

A disadvantage of favouring feeling over dealing is that you often look like you have gone to pieces. This can mean the situation is made worse than it would otherwise have been because you are now coping with two issues – the original issue, plus your massive outpouring of emotion on top of that. One consequence of this can be that others are distracted by having to look after you and your collapse, rather than deal with whatever was wrong in the first place. It also can leave you feeling utterly miserable in the face of what feels like uncontrollable helplessness.

As therapists, asking feelers to 'recognise and stay with the feeling', as one would with a dealer, is completely unhelpful: their issue is being too much in the feeling. What they need to do is learn how to engage the brain and enlist its help in coping with the deluge. That way they don't get flooded to quite the same extent. We are trying to give them control of the tap, so to speak. We want to allow the feelings out in a steady, controllable stream, as opposed to bursting through the walls of a dam and engulfing everyone, feeler and witness alike.

At a very simplistic level, this is another one of the aims of psychotherapy – finding balance. We aim to help the dealers recognise the tendency to shut themselves off from their emotions, and instead help them learn how to get more in touch with their feelings. This enables them to loosen the brain's iron grip so they can gain information from the painful feelings, with the happy consequence they can then more readily experience pleasurable feelings too. And we try to help the feelers spot the signs signalling that they are about to flood and instead bring a bit of control to their emotions, by engaging the mind to do what it does best – calm the situation, acknowledge the feelings, without them running amok and causing chaos.

We also aim to find balance, not just between feeling and dealing, but also between body and mind. We aim to integrate the messages from each, integrating them into a more unified 'bodymind' that ensures that both of these important sources of information get a look-in, so that neither presides to the exclusion of all else. Doing so provides us with more of a choice as to how to react, as opposed to rendering us slaves to our automatic-pilot responses, helpless to stop these taking over and obliterating either half of our bodymind. But as we will see, in times of crisis that is not always so easy to do, no matter how much therapy you have had or how well trained you are in helping clients try to do this for themselves! We therapists do have to acknowledge that sometimes it can often be a case of do as I say, not as I do.

*   *   *

What I do is, I continue 'to do'. That is, in this time of crisis I regress to old ways of coping. I ignore my body, engage my brain, I keep busy, and I deal. I work hard on the mounds of admin that a death produces. I carry on planning the funeral, and I start to compose my eulogy. This I find relatively easy to write because Bill was such an amazing man and I have so much to say about him and all that he meant to me. I have asked members of his family, and some of his best school, university, acting and writing friends, as well as a work colleague, to talk about the various stages of life they shared with him. But I want to write something myself about his more personal life with me.

One night my friend Louise comes for supper, which current babysitter, Sherie, has prepared for us. I am eating again, but only slowly and in small doses. Louise is unable to come to the funeral, as she will be away, so I read them the eulogy. As I reach the end I look up and see that both of them are in tears. I am surprised. I find it hard to understand why they are crying. I feel completely numb and a bit bemused.

'Is it sad?' I ask. I am clearly in denial about why I needed to write this eulogy.

Of course, one part of my brain knows Bill is dead and that I will never see him again, yet the reality of what that actually means and feels like in practice is taking a while to catch me up. This is a strange and disconcerting feeling – a feeling of living two parallel lives at once. There is one where I know he's gone, and then another, far more pleasant one, where he's just not around at the moment. He's away on work. Or he's in another room. And it's not like I'm telling myself that to make myself feel better – one part of my brain really does believe that to be true, that he has just popped out and will be back soon.

In those moments when one world crashes through into the other it's devastating. It's like hearing the news for the first time all over again. When an unbidden realisation such as 'I'll never hear his voice again' pops up and crosses the great divide from the believing brain to the non-believing brain it is like being punched in the stomach. I somehow feel the truth of it viscerally in a way that I just couldn't before. And I want to throw up. And give up. And so the cushion of shock steps back in to save me, wraps itself around me again for a while until the next thought, phrase or image punches me again. And again. And again. It's exhausting. It's painful and destabilising.

Alongside the believing him to be away on work comes habitual behaviour relevant to our relationship as was, making no amendments for the new reality. For instance, I change nothing in the house in case he'll be disorientated or cross when he gets home and sees things moved around. I do the washing-up, so he has a tidy home to come back to. I put my shoes away because it is a long-running bugbear of his that I leave them strewn around the house. I pick up the things I've left on the stairs so he doesn't trip over them if he gets back in the dark. Part of me knows this is nuts and he isn't coming home, but part of me can't take in the finality of it, or function without believing that he must be. I don't know how to not take him into account, his presence is so ingrained in me I don't know how to do otherwise.

~

Another word for what I am doing is of course denial.

Elisabeth Kubler Ross, mentioned earlier, named denial as the first stage in her famous 'five stages of grief' model. So famous is it, in fact, that many people think hers is the only model or theory of grief, and that it is therefore completely true for all those grieving. This is not the case, of course, helpful though it can be to so many. True, a lot of the things I have been describing so far – the shock, the dissociation, the dealing, even my earlier refusal to believe the doctor's warnings in the hospital, my inability to take any of this in – are classic denial symptoms.

So in many ways the Kubler Ross model got it right – denial exists; I lived it. And for me it did indeed come very early on. It was one of my first stages. But it wasn't the only thing that I experienced. There were many other things in the mix too – the meltdowns and the all-too-real and unstoppable waves of grief that at times stormed through that denial.

But – and I can't say this often enough – not everyone will experience it. And of those who do, some might not experience it as a first or only stage. It may come later in the process. Or some of us – the majority in fact – will probably loop in and out of it for a very long time.

Again, this is all part of the essential thing to remember – that there is no right, or normal, way to experience grief. Kubler Ross's stages have a lot of validity and many people, myself included, relate to them. But there will also be much in her theory that doesn't resonate.

Denial is not confined to grief. It is one of many defences that we all tend to employ, to a greater or lesser extent, throughout life. These defences were identified, and named, by Sigmund Freud, and expanded by his daughter Anna. Both Freuds believed that these defences came into being in order to shield ourselves against raging internal, unacceptable urges, often of the murderous or sexual kind.

This notion grew and mutated over the years as Freud's early ideas were built upon and developed further by other theorists. Now it is widely believed that we use defences to guard ourselves against a lot more than just our libidinal drives. When we talk about defences nowadays, we tend to mean those methods we employ, subconsciously, to defend ourselves from a wide range of anxieties or insecurities. From anything about ourselves, in fact, that might be just too painful to face. The use of defences, like denial, or others – repression, regression, displacement, projection, reaction formation, intellectualisation, rationalisation or sublimation – is a protective strategy, but it is also a form of self-deception.

Denial is a way of not accepting the truth of a situation too painful to acknowledge. It's a refusal to experience as real an unacceptable state of affairs, no matter how compelling the evidence of its veracity.

It is extremely hard for the brain to process the stark fact of death, to catch up with reality, so the denial helps us survive the loss by pacing the grief, giving us only so much to bear at any one time. I had to continue acting as though Bill was due home at any time because him being gone for good was not an acceptable state of affairs. I needed him, I wanted him. He had to be coming home because life was not worth living without him. Denial is a much more comfortable place to reside than reality so we do whatever we can to remain there, working hard at preventing painful reality from intruding. We are constructing our defences, and they can come in many forms.

Denial can also take the form of pretending it doesn't matter that the person we loved is gone. We might minimise their importance in our life, underestimate the impact the death is having on us. We may even tell ourselves and others: 'It's not that big a deal, he wasn't that important to me, I managed without him before, I can manage again.' It is all rubbish, of course, but part of us needs to believe it won't have the impact that it absolutely will have.

This form of denial is not dissimilar to one of the other Freudian defences – rationalisation. Rationalisation is a cognitive distortion of the facts, a way of explaining something away by appealing to a logical or rational description, even if that excuse doesn't make sense.

Another one of my own defences is intellectualisation, thinking my way through it. This is a defence particularly employed by the dealers among us, those of us who prefer to live in our heads rather than our bodies. It is no real surprise that I'm choosing to spend time writing this book and thinking about what is going on. If I were to stop, I might actually have to feel something.

In contrast, the defence more often used by the feelers is regression – allowing your more childlike impulses to take over; giving full throttle to your rage, perhaps. Alternatively, you might hide under the duvet, feeling unable to function without someone holding your hand, or propping you up, or stroking your hair.

The defence of sublimation also manifests in me. This is avoiding pain by pouring energy into related activities. For me workaholism has been very much in evidence. I keep the unwelcome thoughts and feelings at bay by keeping on the go, remaining endlessly busy, not allowing a moment of quietness to settle in case that invites the pain of reality or an emotion to get through. Some of the things I have used to hide from reality are sociability – meeting friends – or creating jobs for myself like tidying the house, or losing myself in admin.

More everyday examples of sublimation include things like turning aggressive urges into success in the sporting arena, or using sad or depressive instincts to paint a masterpiece, play or compose music, or write a novel or poem.

Another common form of denial is to anaesthetise yourself via other routes – alcohol or drugs, overeating or undereating, hoarding, cleaning, spending money or gambling – whatever it takes to stay dissociated and thus prevent unbearable reality from intruding.

Like feeling and dealing – themselves, as we have seen, forms of defence – we all have our favoured ways of protecting ourselves and it is important not to be judgemental of ourselves or of someone else going through a crisis. Those defences may manifest very differently in different people but remember that they would not have come into being if there wasn't a very good reason, a wound that needed protecting. It is also important to remain, not just non-judgemental, but also compassionate. None of us would be indulging in any of this if at some point we hadn't been terrified and in need of a security guard, even if we now no longer consciously remember what it was that so scared us. And no one defence is really any 'better' or more emotionally healthy than another, although they may be more physically healthy, or more easily accepted by society.

For instance, many of my friends have been congratulating me on how 'well' I am doing. They claim that if this had happened to them, they would be downing a bottle of wine a night, or refusing to get out of bed, or screaming. The implicit message here being that my busyness, my dealing, my intellectualising, book-writing, all somehow signify that I am coping, whereas they would not. However, just because my form of denial is more productive and socially acceptable, fundamentally it doesn't really make it any healthier on an emotional level, or more honest about what I am really feeling than the person drinking the wine, watching Netflix from under the duvet or endlessly weeping over their friends. Whatever method of denial one experiences, the reason for it is the same – we are all defending ourselves against the pain of feeling the loss.

Another name, mentioned earlier, that sits alongside that of Elisabeth Kubler Ross in the area of grief and loss is William Worden. In 2008 he came up with a model that identified, not five stages as she had done, but four 'tasks'. The first task he identified is 'To accept the reality of the loss'.

Inherent in this 'task' is clearly the implication that reality hasn't been accepted and that the grieving person cannot move forward until it has been. This of course corresponds pretty closely to the notion of denial.

Worden's second task is 'To process the pain of the loss', his third is 'To adjust to a world without the deceased' and his fourth 'To find an enduring connection with the deceased in the midst of embarking on a new life.' They are not quite as snappy or memorable as Kubler Ross's five stages but they do all correspond relatively closely to hers, if with slightly different emphases.

The day of Bill's funeral is a perfect example of how grief has me switching in and out of denial and reality, feeling and dealing. Closely mirroring these dual states of mind, even the day itself is to be split into two. In the morning we will hold a small religious service in the local crematorium. This will give Bill's family and his five closest friends the chance to say goodbye to his coffin in relative intimacy. A buffet lunch back at our house will follow, then there will be a bigger, secular memorial service for our wider friendship group at a local music venue called Bush Hall – a beautifully restored Edwardian music hall that we both love. The theatricality of this feels appropriate given Bill's long association with the theatre world, and it is also somewhere we had briefly considered as a wedding venue all those moons ago. It is also where Bill spent his final evening – he had a been at a gig there the Saturday night before his Sunday collapse.

The day turns out to be not only one of two halves, logistically and emotionally, but also a day featuring some very, and I mean very, weird events; events that my rational brain struggles to take in. These convince me Billy is here with us in spirit, cheering us on, showing his approval and – so that we can be in no doubt that it is he – making us laugh in his own characteristic way.

*   *   *

The first clue we have that Billy is taking part in – directing, even – his own funeral comes midway through the crematorium service. So far this has been a desperately sad morning. From the moment the hearse pulls up outside the house to collect me I find it hard to keep it together. I sob quite uncontrollably throughout the painfully slow drive to the crematorium, and through the first half of the service. But in a move eerily reminiscent of our first meeting – when I had done nothing but cry up to the point Bill started making jokes and I found myself crying with laughter instead – he manages to pull off the same trick here.

The service is led by Graham, a vicar and friend of ours. His gentle speeches are interspersed with moving testimonies and contributions from our close, small group – the singing of a hymn chosen by Bill's sisters, two beautiful eulogies, one each by two of his best friends, Tam and Mike, and the reading of two poems by his two nieces, Poppy and Olive. A third niece, Caitlin, is due to sing 'Any Dream Will Do' from the musical *Joseph*, this being the first of many shows Bill had taken her to see as a child. Caitlin is to be accompanied by Tony, a friend of Bill's, who travelled up from Cornwall this morning to attend both funerals and to play the organ here in the crematorium, and later the piano in Bush Hall.

The moment for the song arrives. Caitlin takes her place by the microphone and Tony presses down on the first key. Nothing happens. He presses and presses and still no sound emerges. We all shuffle a bit in our seats, expectantly waiting as Caitlin looks nervous and Tony looks baffled.

There are a couple of mildly funny comments, at which we all laugh loudly, desperate for light relief. But what happens next makes me feel convinced that Billy has orchestrated things.

He was self-deprecating about his acting career and always liked to poke fun at himself; whenever we were watching telly together and an actor came on in a tiny walk-on part, especially if it was a rather hunched, scruffy or down-at-heel figure, Billy would unfailingly say 'That's my part.'

He also loved to draw humour from little everyday moments and observations and could always weave a funny tale out of something that to most of us would seem nondescript or mundane.

And he could effortlessly defuse a tense situation by saying something like 'What's good about this is that no one's over-reacting' or 'What's good about you is that you are not over-dramatising in any way,' with his trademark deadpan delivery.

This is nothing if not a tense situation. Graham the vicar disappears off behind the scenes to look for someone who might be able to help, while the rest of us continue our shuffling, and snuffling, mild giggles notwithstanding. Eventually a large unkempt figure in a donkey jacket, looking for all the world like an extra in a sitcom, shuffles his way into the room, edges his way around the very obvious coffin that we are all trying to ignore but which sits bang slap in the middle of the space we are gathered around, and makes his way to the organ, hunching down and trying unsuccessfully to pretend he's invisible. He presses a button on the side of the organ, mutters shyly 'It's the master switch', and then reverses his unmissable bulk back across the space, again skirting around the coffin in an exaggeratedly embarrassed fashion as we watch his every step. And as he turns to leave, we can see that he has the word STAFF written in huge letters across the back of the donkey jacket – just the sort of tiny detail Bill would have found hilarious.

'That's Billy's part!' I yell, and we all fall about. It's so exactly his sense of humour and feels just like his classic deflation of a pompous scene; 'What's good about this funeral is that no one's taking any of it too seriously' being the unspoken message.

Once we've settled, the organ sounds its notes, Caitlin sings her showstopper and we all manage to leave the service in a more uplifted mood than the one we arrived in. I feel elated. I am convinced that Billy is there with us, sending his approval.

Thanks in large part to feeling that I have Billy's support and tacit approval, I approach the afternoon's memorial service – hosting upwards of about 300 people – in a very different frame of mind and even feel bold enough to deliver the eulogy myself. I had originally written it with the intention of having it read out by the humanist celebrant, but now I feel buoyed up by the morning's events. Or maybe I'm just all cried out, or maybe it's because I feel so supported by the huge atmosphere of love within the room, or all of the above. Anyway, when it comes to it I ask the celebrant to step down and I get up to speak the words myself.

I speak of how happy Bill made me, how he changed my life, gave me my best fourteen years, and I mean every word. I speak of how much I admire him; how grateful I am to him, and for having had him in my life, even if only for those four-teen years.

And while I don't say this out loud, I can't fail to acknowl-edge just how deep that gratitude runs. Despite our shared and ongoing grief over our lack of children, and our sadness at how separate we are from my family, Bill and I were deter-mined to make the most of what we did have, to appreciate that we had each other, how compatible and in love we were. We shared a worldview, and we shared values. And we were both determined to live life to the full. I couldn't bring myself to share his interest in either sport or beer, and he had no love for my passions of yoga and cooking, but we had a myriad of other hobbies and interests in common.

In these, our shared experiences of painful loss as well as those of making every moment count, I realise now that we were already learning the lessons I am now going to have to try to undertake on my own: the importance of searching out the momentary, everyday joys, the ways of making sadness and longing and loss that tiny bit more bearable by focusing on pleasures that are attainable. Little had I known that this was soon going to stand me in good stead for losing him. Nor had I any concept of how hard doing it alone was going to be.

The wobbly lectern is the only thing keeping me upright. But I have more to say and I want to talk about Bill's adventurous spirit. So I tell the hall about some of the mad exploits we had together: enduring a seven-day fast in Bali during which we drank clay and underwent colonic irrigation; climbing volca-noes in Costa Rica; crashing, then helping manually push, our aeroplane in Fiji. I also told how Bill's short temper and impatience had managed to lead him into heated arguments over a custard tart in Portugal and the width of the train station platform in Shepherd's Bush. His crowning glory was getting us sacked from our own holiday in South Africa, escorted off the premises when he stood up to a bully running a baboon orphanage. He was a man of principles as well as bravery.

I tell of how, soon after getting married, we both took a whole year off from our regular jobs, working as travel journalists and journeying through South-east Asia for three months before spending nine months in Australia.

How, whilst there, he did a diploma in applied psychology while I trained as a yoga teacher. How we'd thought about how we wanted the rest of our lives to unfold. Listening to Bill talk so enthusiastically about the applied psychology he was studying encouraged me to train as a psychotherapist, a decision utterly and wholeheartedly supported by Bill, the most generous person I have ever known. Bill was so supportive it became a bit of a joke. A phrase he used practically every single day, often more than once, was 'that's the best thing you've ever done.' Whether he was referring to me solving some complex problem, or merely finding the ketchup in the fridge that he swore blind wasn't there, he never stopped praising me. Every day I heard 'That's the best thing you've ever done.'

I finish by telling the crowd that I am praying that Bill and I stay in sync wherever he is now and that he will continue to guide me and care for me.

And after I make this plea, Bill answers – I am convinced – by rustling up some more messages for me, the first two through his friend Andy. Andy has talked in his eulogy about the only argument he and Bill ever had in their thirty-year friendship, which concerned whether J. D. Wetherspoon actually exists in person. The day after the funeral, the guest on *Desert Island Discs* is none other than Tim Martin, founder of the J. D. Wetherspoon chain. And Andy also talks about one of the plays he and Bill worked on together, which included a joke about a clue in the *Times* crossword – 'red fruit', to which the answer was 'tomato'. On the day of the funeral, one of the clues and its answer in that day's *Times* crossword was exactly this.

I get goose pimples now, just thinking about these. And it gets weirder. Bill loved the Pretenders, and for the memorial service I had chosen two of their songs. The day after the funeral, our friend Penny was attending the service in her local church and, improbable as it might sound, there, a few pews ahead of her, was none other than Chrissie Hynde, the Pretenders' lead singer. Penny, scattering old ladies in her wake, rushed down the aisle to inform Chrissie that she had been at a memorial service for her friend the day before, and that we had sung two of her songs in his honour.

'Oh, if I'd known I'd have come and sung them for you,' said rock goddess Chrissie Hynde to this slightly deranged stranger. 'Which songs were they?'

The anticlimactic end to this story is that Penny could not remember the titles. This is exactly the sort of absurd humour that Bill would have adored.

What I really want to convey in talking about these things is that whether you believe it to be coincidence or spiritual intervention, reality or fantasy, sanity or madness, these genuinely feel to me like messages from Bill. Psychotherapists who have done research with bereaved people have discovered how common such phenomena are and that those experiencing them seem almost universally to find huge comfort and support in them. As do I. I hug them close and laugh and thank him for staying in touch, and for continuing to make me laugh as he always has done.

I do know he's not actually here, of course I do. It's not the same, and of course it's not enough. But it sure as hell is something, it's all I have now, and I am not letting it go.

Chapter Two

Scattering

I dream I am on the loo in a glass-walled apartment on the highest floor of a tall tower block. Mid-flow I hear a huge explosion, see clouds of dust muddy the clear skies, and know that dynamite buried beneath the tower block has detonated. I feel the reverberations of the shuddering, collapsing building rock my body as I prepare to tumble to my death, knickers round my ankles, amidst the crumbling ruins. I close my eyes and resignedly prepare to meet my fate.

While my waking self continues to revert to 'dealer' type, dealing relatively efficiently with day-to-day practicalities, my sleeping self – when I do manage to get some sleep – experiences its own very different version of dealing. In sleep my unconscious deals with trauma in the best way it knows how – by dreaming. The unconscious is of course another one of the concepts Freud brought into public discourse. It is the notion that underneath those things of which we are consciously aware lies a huge iceberg made up of feelings, drives, memories, wishes and other things we would rather not know about ourselves, things that might contradict the carefully constructed edifice of our public selves. The small tip of this iceberg that is revealed above the waterline belies the enormity of the dense mass beneath. Invisible it may be, yet it exerts huge influence over our waking behaviour. When we sleep it is liberated to express itself in its own more eloquent language, the language of dreams.

When analysing a dream, the first question to consider is the feeling it evokes in the sleeper. The feeling this dream leaves me with is one of relief. I feel a bit scared, but more dominant is a feeling of release. The second thing is to consider the content of the dream. I don't think it requires a huge amount of analysis to see that being on the loo, knickers round my ankles, revealed in this way to the whole world by a glass wall, shows how exposed I feel, and how publicly I feel seen in my vulnerability. But I don't feel ashamed so much as resigned to my powerlessness, accepting of it. The explosion causing my carefully constructed tower to crumble is clearly the edifice of my life being taken out from under me, not with a whimper but with a bang.

I wake from my unsubtle dream and survey the bombsite that my life has become. I recognise the sheer impossibility of picking my way through the ruins unscathed. Sharp stones and massive craters are waiting to trip me up, sprain my ankles and pierce my shoeless feet at every turn. How do I take even one step forward? The largest and closest piece of wreckage right now facing me is how on earth to get through the next few minutes, the next few hours, let alone the three long weeks between now and Christmas, now that I no longer have the distraction of a funeral to plan. I am consumed with dread as to how to navigate a path through these rubble-strewn weeks ahead and cannot even begin to contemplate the gaping hole of Christmas itself.

I agonise over it but decide to go on our pre-booked holiday to St Lucia on my own. I don't want to, but on the other hand an activity holiday filled with water sports and fitness classes seems a suitably distracting, if incongruous, way of keeping busy. If I'm going to be miserable, I might as well be miserable in the sunshine, I reason.

So one week after the funeral I get on a plane, tears streaming down my cheeks. These continue to flow pretty much throughout the entire duration of the twelve-hour flight, and reach their peak when I try to fill in the landing card I've been handed. One of the questions, and goodness knows why this even matters, is 'married or single'. These are the only two options and I am paralysed by them. What am I? I have no idea. Not only does the question metaphorically encapsulate my whole existential dilemma of who on earth I am without Billy, but on a literal level I cannot answer. Bill is dead, so I guess that means I am not married any more. But I still feel married, so I can't bring myself to put single. That feels like a lie and a betrayal. I have no idea what to do. Soon I cannot see through the tears and start to panic that I will pass out from lack of oxygen, so hard is it to breathe. My brain has shut down and my pen just hovers above the form, quivering uselessly in my shaking hand. Twenty minutes or so pass before I clench everything, tick single and shove the hateful card to the bottom of my bag.

Throughout this pathetic performance the woman in the seat next to me resolutely refuses to look at or engage with me in any way. In good old British style she decides to pretend she is not sitting next to a snivelling, shaking, sobbing wreck, and in good old British style I am delighted for this to be the case.

We land and I get a cab to my resort, drained and regretting my decision to come. I go straight to bed.

I wake to a beautiful view and beautiful weather.

'So fucking what?' I ask myself. 'What does it bloody matter?'

I find it painful to acknowledge the beauty of the sun-drenched, sweeping bay of shimmering water in front of me. I also cannot envisage how I could possibly take part in any of the activities that are meant to be diverting me. My body feels like a lead weight, incapable of any movement more strenuous than dragging itself over to the breakfast buffet.

But what to do when the distraction of shovelling food in my face is over? From the deep recesses of my brain I dredge up the knowledge that journaling is meant to be a good resource when in emotional distress. Without my friends there to talk to, I decide to write my way through the pain instead. I grab my laptop and head out to the beach. When I settle and begin, I am surprised by what comes out from under my furiously typing fingers:

I'm such a fucking idiot. Two months ago I thought I was having an existential crisis. Well now I'm well and truly staring a fucking existential crisis in the face. I'm 49 years old and I've lost my best friend, the only person I ever truly loved and was loved by, the only person who can really make me laugh and keep me safe.

It is unbelievable to think that until five weeks ago I really thought my life was hard. I thought that the approach of my fiftieth birthday, with menopause, childlessness, ageing and lack of purpose weighing heavily, I had cause enough for self-pity and angst. I had had no idea what was about to hit me, and I now don't know whether to laugh or cry at how naïve, uncomprehending and innocent I was then.

Now here I am sitting on a fucking paradisiacal Caribbean beach with a view – I was going to say 'to die for' except that Bill actually did, so that doesn't feel right. Let's say instead: a view that wows. If I were capable of being wowed that is.

A smiling waiter has just offered me a Popsicle. A free one. I normally never knowingly turn down a free ice cream, or in fact a free anything, particularly if it contains sugar and fat in combination, but I cannot fit anything else into my extended belly, having gone a bit overboard at the buffet – also free – at this posh luxury hotel that Bill and I chose three months ago as a pre-Xmas pick-me-up. It was the most expensive holi-day we'd ever booked – a 'fuck you' to Brexit and Trump, and the death of Bill's mother, and our mutual existential crisis in the face of a world gone mad and our inability to find our place in it. To hell with being sensible and frugal, we'd said, let's start to live a bit. Let's spend money. Let's book an expen-sive holiday. Life is short, the apocalypse is coming, the pound will soon be worthless, America will soon be at war with North Korea, the ice caps will melt, before too long there will be no expensive Caribbean islands above sea level left to visit, so what are we waiting for? Let's start to live.

And yet he didn't. He did the exact opposite. He stopped living.

In between deciding to live life to the full by booking an expensive holiday, and me actually coming on said holiday, he bloody died. And if I'm saying it over and over, it's because I'm still trying to make it sink in. Because it still hasn't. Despite the days spent sitting next to him in his coma in hospital, despite seeing his waxen corpse in a bamboo coffin in the funeral home, despite a funeral and a memorial service and a solitary flight to a single room in the Caribbean, and the tears rolling unstoppably down my cheeks, it still doesn't feel real. It still feels completely impossible.

Why am I too full for the free Popsicle delivered direct to my sunlounger? Because during said buffet breakfast I not only chose and ate all the things I wanted, I also piled up all the things Bill would have chosen, and I ate them too. I feel absolutely furious with the chefs here for being so callous as to make and display all his favourite foods when he cannot be here to eat them. Bloody bread and butter pudding, which he adored. What's that even doing on a Caribbean menu? Never mind him missing out on thirty more years of love and creativity and joy and experiences, I can't bear to think of him not getting the bread and butter pudding that he would have been so enthusiastically, vocally happy about. So I feel duty-bound to eat it on his behalf. And I don't even like bread and butter pudding. And I'm wearing a bikini. And I'm nearly fifty. It's not a good combo. Do I care? Not really. Do I care about anything any more? No. I've been robbed. Not as badly as he's been robbed, obviously, I can still eat bread and butter pudding, which he can't, but still robbed. Of the love of my life, of the future we had ahead of us. Of any joy or hope or faith in the world. Or indeed any clue as to who I am now or what I'm going to do with this life I no longer want.

I continue scribbling frantically: 'I've come to paradise to experience hell. It feels incongruous to say the least.' I pause and realise how much anger is fizzing off the page. I have a light-bulb moment – oh, so this is what Kubler Ross meant when she described anger as one of the stages of grieving. Now, I understand it. It's not just that you are angry that the person has died, you actually ARE anger. Your whole body is full of it, anger, rage, resentment, hate, all of it steaming out of every pore. Or at least that's how I feel. Yes, some of it is being directed out at specific things and people, waiters and chefs and happy holidaymakers and the beautiful view, but some of it is just all-pervasive. I cannot separate myself from the anger. I am glowing with it, vibrating with it. I hate the world and everything and everyone in it, myself included.

I suddenly realise I am thinking like a therapist, observing and registering and being curious about what is going on for me, even while another part of me is in the grip of feeling it. I wonder if this will be useful. I wonder if I could possibly try to write down a sort of conversation between my 'therapist self' and my 'grieving self' and see where it takes me, whether it will help me process what's going on, give me some perspective.

And then I have the corollary thought that maybe this could be useful not just to me. Maybe having a little bit of insider knowledge of what the theories really feel like might also be useful to my future clients. I feel momentarily cheered by this thought, that I can put this horror show to some use. But even this vaguely hopeful glimmer immediately turns sour in my mind. Will I have future clients? Can I even continue to work as a psychotherapist when I feel so sad and alone and collapsed? Without a strong, loving person propping me up from behind, how can I hope to prop anyone else up? And on a practical level, can I afford to do a relatively poorly paying job if I am the sole income earner? As always my fears veer from emotional distress to the practicalities of losing Bill and back again, all within a vortex of confusion and seething anger.

Great. Now I can add potentially not having a career to return to onto my list of things to be furious about.

~

When I talk about 'therapist me' and 'grieving me' I don't see this only as a mind/body dialectic, or a feel/deal dialectic. The notion that we are made up of many different selves is part of a psychotherapeutic model known by various names, 'subpersonalities' being one and 'configurations' another.

The idea of multiple selves, different personalities, all of which reside within and make up our external character, is a more nuanced variation on Donald Winnicott's theory of true and false selves.

Many people, whether they've heard of Winnicott or not, instinctively feel they have a 'real' or 'true' self, hidden deep behind all the layers of social constructs and patterning that have built up over the years. They long to find 'the real me' and this search is often what drives them into therapy.

I am more inclined towards the other theories – and there are a few different variations on this subject – that suggest we are not just one true self, hidden by a false one. Instead we are made up of many different internal selves, all of which represent equally 'true' aspects of ourselves, and all of which serve a purpose.

For instance, there may be the 'go-getting self' who interviews well and climbs the career ladder and makes sure there is money coming in. She may reside alongside an 'insecure self' who can't talk to an attractive love object without blushing and stammering, or a 'bullshitter self' who greets either scenario – job interview or first date – by swaggering with bravado to pre-emptively counteract an assumed rejection. These may well share the space with a 'frightened self' terrified of being alone, or of disappointing a strict parent.

We can be all these things and more; the options are endless. Each self, whether it be welcome or not, comfortable to experience or not, healthy and useful or not, allowed out in public or not, nevertheless represents an equally valid and true part of our make-up. It's just that each manifests in different situations and for different reasons. Some of our selves we love, some we hate. Some we can acknowledge, some we cannot.

This theory speaks to me strongly, and I use this model of different selves a lot in my therapeutic practice. I offer my clients the analogy that our many different personalities are like characters in a play. And that sometimes one character starts to take over and hog the spotlight, causing the others to feel left out. Sometimes their dissatisfaction reaches a point where their mutterings and complaints can be heard on stage, and so start to distract and put off the leading lady, who starts to forget her lines or needs to shout louder to make herself heard.

I love the theatre, so this analogy works for me. But if my clients are more musical, then I will perhaps instead use a different analogy – that our selves are like the different members of an orchestra that can only sound harmonious if each instrument respects the other and doesn't play too loudly, or too often, or demand its own rhythm. Visually minded people might prefer thinking of their different selves as different colours in a spectrum, and how the picture can get overwhelming – or too boring – if too much red is used at the expense of any blue or yellow. You get the idea.

Living with a discordant team of players all vying for attention and throwing the whole cast off balance is another reason people seek therapy. Many of us have got so stuck in one, unhelpful way of being – the successful careerist for instance – that our other selves never get a look-in, never get their moment in the spotlight. Instead, these other selves – maybe our vulnerable, or creative, or rebellious selves – are left waiting in the wings, getting more and more resentful and bitter. Then what can happen is that the more dominant self, normally so in control, starts to lose confidence and stability. Disorientation ensues. Who actually am I? Why do all my old certainties suddenly feel so less, well, certain? Why does my successful career that used to feel so important suddenly seem more like a prison than a podium? Again, the variations are endless.

Looked at in this way, I can see that there on the beach my own myriad selves are doing battle for the spotlight: 'Unhappy, confused self' has been hogging centre stage for quite some time now. Meanwhile 'dealer self' is doing vocal exercises in the wings. She's ready to make her entrance to counsel that I won't always feel like this, that I might want to go back to work one day, and that I can get support if so, but that it's also okay if I choose not to do that.

But this sensible, reassuring advice from a mature, rational version of me is soon overwhelmed by a rather less grown up, positively teenage 'angry self' entering stage right. It's almost as though she machine-guns the 'grown-ups' off the stage and proceeds to kick the whole set down, sending the others running for cover.

'Fuck right off with being rational, this is fucking shit and I don't deserve it and I hate the world and everyone in it!' Right now anger is definitely winning the battle to control today's script.

If I look at my grief from this perspective, then perhaps my 'therapist self' is more of an observer – the play's director perhaps, or the orchestra's composer. From a position in the auditorium she has a wider, more objective viewpoint as to what is going on up there on stage. Here she can stay one tiny part removed from the agony that the other parts are experiencing and offer some stage direction, making sure no one gets more airtime than the others, that no one monopolises the story, no one feels so excluded they cause chaos backstage, chaos that one day will reach such a fever pitch that it spills over onto the stage. She can hopefully start to untangle the growing cacophony of voices and egos currently tantrumming away on stage, so that they can eventually work together as a harmonious company, as opposed to a maelstrom of competing egos. And most importantly, she needs to help them make room for the newest member of the cast – the 'bereaved self', the one experiencing the pain, the grief, the terror. The one who feels she wants to call time on this fiasco and burn down the whole theatre, raze it to the ground and so end the whole sorry mess.

An important aim in therapy – and the aim of 'therapist me' right now – is to start to work from a more integrated place, a place where warring selves don't elbow each other off the stage. At some, for me currently impossible to imagine, future point, they will once again work as an ensemble cast, encouraging, supporting and being generous to one another, each having their moment in the spotlight when needed.

This book is in many ways the result of me trying to listen in to each of my characters: letting them tell their stories and their different, sometimes contradictory methods of getting through this tragedy; trying to make sense of why they act as they do; and exploring what they need to feel that their time on the stage is productive, fair and fulfilling.

Right now it seems 'sad me' is pushing to take over the spotlight from 'angry me' and is demanding to have her moment. She takes her cue.

I'm on one of the exceedingly comfortable sunloungers on the exceedingly beautiful beach looking at an impossibly clear sea and I'm crying behind my sunglasses.

I've again just come from breakfast, which like everything in this damn place was horrific in its loveliness. I chose from the vast array of delicious offerings but felt the enormous emptiness that no amount of tropical fruit and made-to-order pancakes was ever going to fill. Acknowledging another huge hole and lack in my life – not being able to discuss my choices, or anything, with my Billy ever again. Talking about food was something we loved doing ('loved!', God, will I ever get used to talking about him in the past tense? It feels so wrong) and would spend (bloody past tense again, tripping me up) hours doing.

Now I was alone with no interest in what I was eating, just shovelling it in mindlessly, and without him there in person I instead held an imaginary conversation with him in my head. And when the conversation dried up it was hard to hide from how terribly, terribly sad I was. And then less welcome chat would enter my head. Phrases I didn't want to hear kept echoing round and round in my head, stark and brutal and – finally – undeniable.

'He is dead.'

'He is gone.'

'I am never going to see him again.'

Impossible to believe the reality of it; the finality of it. And it's not just these horrible, unbelievable words popping in unwelcome and unbidden. There are images too. Flashbacks to what he looked like in the hospital, when he was at least still breathing – albeit only thanks to a machine – and in the funeral home, when he wasn't. And the images are now accompanied by the sensation – the feel of my face against his chest, moving in tandem as that rhythmic rise and fall lifted and lowered my head as I squished myself alongside him in the narrow hospital bed. Sandwiched against the safety bars and trying to avoid lying too heavily on all the wires that were keeping him alive and digging in to my flesh, hearing the machines whirring and beeping, the clatter of medical staff coming in and out, pressing buttons, monitoring digital read-outs, I nevertheless here found a modicum of peace. As I lay with my head on his chest, the last time I would ever experience my skin touching his skin, would ever again have any physical proximity at all in fact, and I talked to him about us. About how much I was going to miss him, about . . .

No, can't do it. Can't think about it. Too upsetting. I fear a collapse may be imminent. I drag myself back from the over-whelming sadness such memories haul up from the depths of my guts. 'I drag myself'? No, I don't have enough autonomy for that. I am not in control. Denial is competing with memory as to what I think about when. I'm not sure who is running this show right now, but I do know I'm a mess.

Whatever I do, an internal running commentary talks me through where Bill would have been at any given moment on this holiday: he would have got up at the crack of dawn and gone running, training for his third marathon; he would have overeaten at breakfast; he would have then complained about having overeaten; and, still complaining at his lack of will-power, he would have staggered over to a sunlounger, fallen asleep, and I would have been cross with him for 'wasting' the morning asleep. I would have done the opposite and run around manically trying to do as many activities as possible, rushing back to him between each one to tell him what I'd done and what I'd thought of it, and trying to persuade him to try them too.

And finally he would have woken up properly, tried to calm me down, said he just wanted to sit quietly, until finally gathering his energy and setting off to his own choice of activity while I collapsed from exhaustion.

But none of this happened. Instead I finished my solitary breakfast and made my solitary way to the beach to find sunloungers all set up in pairs, with a table and umbrella between each. A nice man runs over carrying towels and starts to lay them out on the sunlounger. Bill would have loved this personal service. The running commentary of his voice is saying, in just that way of his, 'I love it here, I love it' and 'This is the best thing you've ever done, bringing us here.'

The smile creeping on to my face as I hear his voice so clearly in my head is soon wiped right off: 'Will there be anyone joining you?' asks the no-longer-quite-so-nice man as he makes to lay the second towel on the second sunlounger. I find myself unable to speak as the realisation dawns that I will never again have Billy next to me on a sunlounger. Or anywhere else. That I am now that rather sad-looking solitary, ageing person with her book and headphones. And hankies.

Of course it's ridiculous that five weeks since he died I am still only just taking in things like the full frontal fact of 'he's dead' and I am alone. But shock and denial are really effective and long-lasting tranquillisers. For a while at least, until real life crashes back through the barrier.

I ask for a glass of water but am in the lavatory when it arrives. I return to find a different waiter has put a bottle of water and two glasses in an ice bucket next to me. Again, the assumption is that of course I would soon be joined by someone. Who would come on a holiday like this alone?

I hear Bill's voice asking more of his familiar stock questions: 'Are you enjoying your holiday, Bats?'

Of course, he would use his pet nickname for me, another thing gone for good. No one else calls me that. And why would they? It's nonsensical; he just liked playing with words and sounds, and to him finding a word that worked with my surname meant that the name Bats Bates had a pleasing ring to it.

'What's your favourite thing about the holiday, Bats?'

Correct and expected answer of course – 'You are, darling!'

He always asked and I always answered thus – but only after I'd first listed the food, and the sun, and the sea, and the massage, and so on. And, as always, he would do his mock-horror reaction at being so low down the list. Every couple has similar stupid, unfunny in-jokes and repetitions that they trot out. They represent that shorthand of familiarity, which seems so silly on the surface but has a deeper unsaid but understood meaning – I love you, I know you, we work in harmony, we complete each other.

Oh go on, give me the bloody Popsicle then. No, no one is bloody joining me, no one loves me, no one cares that I have put on about a stone in weight and am spilling out of my bikini and have already eaten so much I feel sick. The inability to eat that plagued those early days in hospital has all too rapidly been replaced by an inability to stop eating – another tried and tested form of feelings avoidance. Yet the anaesthetising qualities of my carb-based breakfast are already wearing off, so why not stretch my uncomfortably overstretched belly yet further? It might even make me so disgustingly sated that I fall asleep and can enjoy a few minutes of blissful oblivion, something still denied me during the sleepless nights.

*   *   *

Bad though this day has been, the evening proves to be even worse. I walk past the bar and see others enjoying the sunset and the live music, drinks in hand. I visualise all too easily – can see in front of me – the alternative reality that should have been: Bill and me sitting among them, him with his beer and me with the cocktail he would have encouraged me to have.

Instead I walk on past, knowing that sitting alone at one of those beach tables with their flickering candles is an impossibility. I am trying not to think about him, but my thoughts are very disobedient, and they do stray far more often than I would like. Except not thinking about him is horrible too. The guilt. How dare I not think about him? What betrayal. What a terrible wife I am. Was. Shit.

I'm not a big drinker but at supper I try the cocktails, downing them like a nutter. I know Bill loved the rare occasions when I let go and drank. But really, what does it matter now? Drunk, hungover, sober, I can't really feel any worse than I do already, so who cares?

Solitary, rushed supper negotiated, I move on to the loneliness of the bedroom. When I put on the light on the far side of the bed, I say to myself, 'I'll put Bill's light on.' Or if I need to prop myself up better to read I say, 'I'll use Bill's pillow.' He's never been in this room but it's still his side of the bed, his pillow, his bedside light. I can't imagine it ever not being.

As usual, it is my 'sad self' who puts herself to bed to lie alone staring at the ceiling, trying to keep the restless thoughts at bay while counting the hours till dawn.

~

What I am realising about grief is how hard it is to convey in words, even to oneself.

This makes it hard to share with others, and even harder to write about. It feels impossible to label or describe. It's a visceral, whole body, whole life, whole attitude, non-verbalisable experience.

I'm finding that these strange, unknown, overwhelming feelings are best described in metaphor, symbolism or imagery. Somehow visualisations give a better sense of this otherworldly, parallel universe I inhabit. The crumbling tower of my night-time dream language is replaced during the day by a recurring visualisation in which the safe ship that was Bill and me has imploded. Smashed into smithereens, a destructive shower of lethal shards of wood and glass is now being hurled around by a raging storm. It has left me thrashing below the surface of a dark and menacing ocean, unsure which way is up, helpless prey to the viciously splintered detritus raining down from above, ready to pierce me below the surface. I'm caught in a massive, bubbling tsunami, my life shattered and now scattered and buffeted by the pounding, relentless waves.

There have been times in the past when I've swum in the ocean and I've timed things wrong and been dumped by a massive wave. I've found myself violently tumbled and turned as though in a washing machine that's churning me over and over until I lose hope and nearly lose consciousness. That is what the last few weeks have felt like: trapped below the surface while tidal waves toy with me, tossing me every which way, as they ready themselves to lift then drop me head first from a great height. My body is pummelled, battered, no longer my own, and my life regularly flashes before my eyes. I am sure I will drown, and just pray that it will be quick so this beating will be over. Occasionally I pop back up for rasping, gasping slugs of air snatched in the few seconds granted me before the next wave hits. But most of the time I surrender helplessly to the inevitable disorientation and terror.

All I hope for in this moment is that the waves may one day get less violent, that the gaps between each rising swell may get longer, and that I may be able to gulp a fraction more oxygen into my lungs each time I fight to the surface. But I do wonder whether I will ever see the shore or feel solid ground beneath my feet again. Right now, this really doesn't feel like a possibility, which in itself unearths another intense feeling – fear. The fear 'Can I survive this?', and, more terrifyingly, 'Do I want to survive this?'

While my feeling self is doing battle within the tsunami-churned waters of my metaphorical world, my physical self is struggling to appreciate the contrastingly calm waters of the material world. I force myself to go for a real-world swim in this beautiful St Lucian bay. I plunge, try to appreciate the warm water on my tensed-up body, and start to swim. I swim towards the horizon. I continue to swim towards the horizon. What I may find there feels no more unknown or frightening than what awaits me on land. I start to wonder: what if I just keep going? It feels an appealing prospect, to swim so far out that coming back is no longer an option, to not have to make any decisions ever again. The choice as to whether to go on – with any of it – would be taken from me and I could just give up. The desire to do this is huge, like a watery version of vertigo – that weird feeling when you are on a high building and you just want to throw yourself off.

What stops me? Two things. Firstly, knowing Bill would be furious with me, for squandering a life he would have loved to have been able to have but was denied.

And secondly, the realisation that I can't do that to the friends who have worked so hard to keep me going these last few weeks. They would think that they hadn't worked hard enough, hadn't loved me enough, and I couldn't bear that because truly they have been unbelievable. No one could have done more. Right from that awful, middle-of-the-night phone call from the hospital telling me that all hope was gone, I have been cradled by extraordinary women. At the crack of dawn on that following morning Julia and Mariana had appeared in front of me. I don't even recall phoning or texting them with the news, but I must have done, and somehow, in less than eight hours, and overnight, they had organised and rearranged their children, their clients, their whole lives and got themselves all the way across London to be with me. Jess, making her way from Bristol, arrived hot on their heels. They, and the others who rallied to my cause, did not leave my side till I came here to St Lucia. And now that I am here they have taken it in turns to Skype me every single day, checking in on me and sending love and support. One friend, Louise, even came to see me here in person, driving miles across the island, temporarily leaving her own holiday on the other coast on the very day she flew in, jet lag ignored.

And all these amazing friends, I know, are going to be there waiting for me when I get home. They are the water wings keeping me afloat, and which now help me, albeit reluctantly, to turn around and swim back to shore to face whatever unimaginable horrors await me there.

If only my spell in the metaphorical tumultuous, tsunami-battered ocean could be so easily exited.

~

After the strangest week I will ever spend on a beach, I return home. If home is still what it is?

This house came into being at the same time as our relationship – during that extraordinary week in Skyros when I met Bill and exchanged contracts on the house. For six short weeks it had been, briefly, *my* house, but with that reckless but right decision to throw our lot in with each other, we turned it into *our* home. Home and Bill having become synonymous, I approach my return there with trepidation.

Fourteen years ago I had chosen the house and the location, so it was only fair that Bill should have some say in what could become of it next. Together we hatched a plan to knock down several internal walls, build a two-storey extension and extend the attic. It became practically a whole new house and we spent many months living in a building site – camping out in the new attic room as soon as it was complete, while the rest of the house was destroyed around us, walls sledgehammered, and floors levered up. All in order that we could create something new together – the first of many joint projects to come, both of the concrete and the more abstract kind.

I was directing C4's architecture series, *Grand Designs*, at the time, so I spent my days filming building sites, then came home to sleep in one. Dust in every pore became a natural state of being. But we were really happy, so excited to have found each other and to be embarking on this joint project together.

And we lived in that same house till the day we headed out for the hospital. Neither of us had any idea that this would be the last time he ever set foot there, the last time we'd ever do anything together, as a couple, again.

So, if being in St Lucia was hard, being at home is harder. I don't know how to create normality in a distinctly un-normal world. How can I make a house for two into a house for one; make a lifestyle predicated on two into a lifestyle for one? It is impossible not to see him in every room, on every chair, in the shower, in the bath, at the sink, in the bed. Memories are stained into every corner, every bit of fabric, every piece of art, every decision ever made about the place. He is there in every meal eaten at that table, every television show watched, every book read on the bookshelves.

Everything that my eye falls upon deals a sucker punch to the face or stomach. It's like the *Batman* comics of my youth. Bill's favourite mug that lies unused on the shelf – pow! His bottles of beer in the fridge that will remain undrunk as I can't stand the stuff – whack! The unfinished book on his bedside table whose ending he will never discover – kersplatt! The half-watched TV series that I now watch alone, trying not to notice how much I miss his never-failingly funny commentary or even how much I miss his annoying habit of endlessly pausing the action to get more snacks or drinks – thwack! The punches keep coming until I am on the floor again, beat.

Every noise I hear sounds as though Bill is arriving home, or emptying the dishwasher, or talking to the cats. How can I possibly ever get used to the silence and space left behind? Everything had been ours, now it is mine. Everything was we, now it is I. I miss him with every bite of a meal, every departure or arrival through a front door that no longer represents safety but alienation, every bedtime and every waking-up. Those are the worst times of day: going to bed knowing I will not sleep, that there is an empty space beside me that I am going to have to lie next to for the next seven or eight hours, the next twenty or thirty years. A cold, flat, lifeless expanse of sheets and duvet, an un-flattened pillow. Yet the few minutes of sleep I do get are worse, because they mean I will have to wake up again, necessitating a re-remembering of what happened, re-losing him all over again as my brain catches up with the new reality of life without him. I am distraught, bereft, uncomprehending, flattened – unlike those tauntingly plumped-up pillows on his side of the bed.

So, practical (dealer) me takes the pillows away and moves my own to the centre of the bed, hoping that will prove less of a daily reminder of his absence. But no, that's worse. That's erasing him, that's removing the evidence of his presence, an acknowledgement that he isn't coming back. There is no way to win this game against grief. There is no hiding from it, no shortcuts. Whatever I do or don't do – face the evidence, hide the evidence, run away from the evidence – grief always finds me. The only way through it is through it. And that is a fucker. The pain is indescribable. I fear I will die from pain this bad. I *hope* I will die from pain this bad. I am exposed, vulnerable, attacked from within by my own psyche.

And that appears to be a psyche still struggling with moments of disbelief, still fearing for my sanity. I pick up the stuff I've left on the stairs in case he slips on it in the dark. I put my shoes away so that he won't, as is his wont, complain about how many pairs are littering the floor. I'm messy, he isn't. Wasn't. Now that I can leave anything I want, anywhere I want and have no one to take into account, I feel oppressed by such freedom. I long for him to complain about my mess so I can feel aggrieved about having to clear it.

But he can't complain. And he also can't help. I empty the dishwasher and it dawns on me that I will always have to empty the dishwasher from now on. This was his job – I did the cooking, he did the clearing up, and now I have to do everything. And of course, the tears that sprout at this realisation are not about having to unload the dishwasher. They're about recognising that it is in these little, everyday moments that the bigger things are symbolised. It's about recognising my existential aloneness via all the concrete things that I will have to tackle alone from now on – from clearing up my own mess, to watching telly, to taking the cats to the vet, to moaning about Brexit, to going on holiday, to mopping up my own tears alongside the dishes. Never again can I snuggle into bed with my best friend and talk over the day, seeking the trusted opinion of the person who knows me best in the world and whose advice I respect. Never again can I flop on the sofa, tired, and know that someone else will take care of things, and of me. No one will say 'You're tired, let me do it,' or 'You stay there, I'll make you a cup of tea.' I need to make my own cups of tea from now on if I want them; need to calm my own inner scream of pain and misery. Anything I need or want from now on, I will have to be proactive in order to effectuate. Nothing is shared – not the good, not the bad.

Just as we had slowly created the house, so we had slowly created our relationship, learning about each other, and of course about ourselves. When I saw myself through Bill's eyes I saw a completely different person from the one I thought I was. Back in those early days, as the walls of the house were dismantled and others built in their place, as it changed its shape around us to became a home and a refuge, so too did our burgeoning relationship bounce against and test its boundaries, renegotiate its limits, lose and create space, and thereby settle into something comfortably and wonderfully home-like. Bill was my safety and stability and security.

~

Feeling safe, stable and secure are now generally seen as essential components for good mental health, but it wasn't always this way. It took an incredible thinker and psychotherapist – John Bowlby – to put these at the heart of psychotherapeutic theory, and like Freud's modelling of our internal world before him, it was a game-changer.

Freud's discoveries and the theories he made about the human psyche, and the reasons about why we behave as we do, were revolutionary. They included concepts that we take for granted today, such as the existence of the unconscious and the theory of defences. Before long, his once-radical ideas started being disseminated, accepted and understood more widely. His protégés started to use what they had learned from him in their own work. They began gathering their own data and thinking more independently as they saw the effects of this way of working on their clients. Many of them began expanding and developing Freud's nascent theories.

The problem was that Freud didn't necessarily always see his theories as nascent, something to be built upon as knowledge grew. He felt that he had pretty much created an unquestionable blueprint of the human mind, which was not to be tampered with by these upstarts. This led to his falling out with many of the people he had trained and been close to. Many of them went on to spawn new, complex theories of their own – for example, Carl Jung obviously developed Jungian theory; Alfred Adler created Adlerian theory, while a rather diverse grouping founded what came to be known as the object relations school. This diverse group included Melanie Klein, Ronald Fairbairn and Donald Winnicott. They didn't always agree on everything and held some contradictory views, but they did all agree that Freud's model of focusing purely on internal drives formed only part of the story. The object relations school took his ideas to another dimension, adding the then equally radical notion that what goes on between people in the outside world (interpersonally) is just as important as what goes on within their own minds (intrapsychically). They realised that relationships are central to our lives, and that they impact and influence our development just as much as the internal world explored by Freud.

Into this changing landscape came another radical thinker, John Bowlby, whose research led him to understand that a child's need for relationship is as fundamental and intrinsic a need as those for food and shelter. He realised that infants are primed to love and to be loved, and that this is a primary need in and of itself, not simply a by-product of what Freud had called the libidinal urges.

In the 1930s Bowlby worked as both a psychiatrist and a psychoanalyst, but it was his work with emotionally disturbed children that led to him developing 'attachment theory', a way of thinking about the human psyche and human development that has become massively influential.

Attachment theory is complex but at its heart Bowlby's theory suggests that we come into the world primed for relationship, and that the quality of early relationships with our attachment figures determines how we will attach to them, and later to others. These ways of attaching were then categorised in different ways, but primarily they were deemed to be either a secure or an insecure attachment, and it was thought that whichever type they were could determine the type and the quality of all our future relationships. Whether, how and to whom we attach is determined in infancy and depends mainly on our primary caregivers. But our attachment style can also be altered later in life. Other attachment figures, such as a teacher, godparent, grandparent, therapist or romantic partner, can also help us to become more attached and consequently more secure. And why is this necessary? Well, for all sorts of reasons, but fundamentally, developing what Bowlby called a 'secure base' is the anchor that allows us to grow and develop a sense of self and of self-esteem, and influences how we manage loss. To be securely anchored in this way also gives us the safety to explore, expand our horizons, and feel safe enough to push boundaries and fulfil our potential.

You may well have a sense of who, for you, represents your secure base now and in the past, and how this has affected you over time. Bill was mine. Knowing he was there for me, no matter what, gave me the confidence to spread my wings and explore and expand my internal and my external world, literally and metaphorically. He allowed me to discover who I was and what I needed. Without my beloved attachment figure no one and nothing is safe, and my world and my confidence has shrunk accordingly.

Chapter Three

Flailing

With my secure base uprooted, where does that leave me? Untethered and floundering, is where – still flailing around in the ocean depths. Or at least that is the metaphor currently tormenting me. I guess it is a step better than when I felt I was being tossed and tumbled by the tsunami – I can now at least keep my head above water for increasingly longer fragments of time, even if my feet are still frantically paddling below the surface, and my eyes desperately seeking dry land on the horizon but finding none.

Winter is well and truly here now, the December days getting colder, shorter and darker, reflecting my mood. Although technically well heated, the house metaphorically provides no warmth or comfort. Without Bill it is no longer really a home. Uncoupled from my secure base, I feel unstable, lonely, scared – the list of grim-sounding, winter-appropriate adjectives is endless, yet none seem to adequately express how lost I feel. As to who or what I am now, I have no idea. I have given up my therapy practice for the time being, and I gave up my television career long ago, but this identity crisis goes far deeper than any label or job description. I am genuinely bewildered as to how to be in this world without Bill, my clichéd 'other half'.

My newly confused sense of self heightens how lonely I am, how my every attempt at communication feels like howling into a bottomless abyss. For fourteen years I have told Bill every single thing that has happened to me – from voicing my deepest darkest fears and insecurities, to recounting the most trivial aspects of my day. And still I try to do so, daily, sometimes hourly. I reach for my phone so I can hear his voice before staring at it uselessly for a moment and placing it back down unused. I call 'Hello, I'm home' as I open the front door, and an empty hallway echoes it back. I cry 'Billy, I've stubbed my toe' into an uncaring void. I text 'I've bought bread' and see letters appearing then immediately disappearing as I remember and have to delete each one instead.

Nothing is too small or too large for me to want to tell him: 'I'll be home late; I've seen a new restaurant you'd love; the guy you like in the newsagent's has left and the new woman is grumpy; I'm terrified and I ache and I miss you and I don't know who I am or what to do; Londis has had a refit; that's the actress from that show we like, you know the one, with thingy from thingy; I am dying inside, a dry husk; the cat has thrown up on the carpet.'

I am going through the biggest crisis of my life and I cannot tell him anything about it. He cannot show interest in the trivialities that were as much a part of the fabric of his life as mine, and he cannot reassure me about the big stuff. I feel desperately alone, which is strange because I am surrounded constantly by people. By my favourite people in the world in fact, all of whom are fantastic listeners; but they are not him, and they cannot really pretend to care who staffs the newsagent's these days, willing though they are to try to go the extra mile with anything I ask.

There is always someone with me, to spend the evening and stay the night. I am profoundly grateful and seriously doubt I would be surviving any of this without this army of incredible women. But nothing can take away from the fact that however much I adore them, and I do, they are not HIM. I'm missing the 'him-ness' of him.

All couples have ways of doing things that are unique to us, that are born out of a shared growth from the years spent entwining around each other's thoughts and habits until they become as inseparable as two plants grafted together. So, although I love my friends, and don't want them to leave, having them in the house is bitter-sweet. Their presence only serves to highlight Bill's absence. Their presence glaringly reflects back how much easier and more comfortable life was with him: the shared language, shared worldview, shared way of stacking the dishwasher. Other people, try as they might, are all just a bit, well, wrong. They don't sit on the sofa the same way, watch telly with just the right amount or quality of commentary, don't have the same balance of silence to chat, humour to seriousness, the same body clock synchronisation. I become self-conscious with the dear friends who keep me company. Should I pause the TV if they talk, or keep going? Do they like the lights on or off when watching? Do they like to eat in front of the telly or beforehand? I've become awkward in my own home because it no longer runs like the super-efficient machine that the Bill–Sasha combo had become, that needed no explanation or thought. It's like when you learn to drive and you have to think about changing gear but soon it becomes so unconscious you're not really even aware you're doing it. In my daily routine I'm back to noticing the gears and having to think about when and how to change them. I become hyper-aware of everything I do because I'm watched, seen in a way that you aren't when with your partner who knows your habits as well as their own and so doesn't even register them. Instead I have to chat, and explain, and be nice. Oh, for Billy to be here so we could be a bit grumpy together, so I wouldn't have to be grateful and polite and friendly, and instead could revert to type and just be a bit of a miserable slob like we always were together, collapsing gratefully, and silently, onto the sofa for a bit of Nordic noir at the end of a stressful day.

When you are surrounded by all your favourite people, whose only aim is to look after you and try to make you feel better, and yet you still feel lonely, it brings the horrible realisation that this is a loneliness that can never be alleviated. Others have expressed it better than I. Julian Barnes calls what he feels in the wake of his wife's death not loneliness but her-lessness; while in her wonderful and moving book about the death of her own husband, author Decca Aitkenhead says that in grief there are plenty of people to do something with, but what's hard is that there is no one to do nothing with. And that really resonates. I would rather have him being annoying than them being nice. And yet that feels ungrateful because I couldn't exist without them either. I want them, but I want him more. Life now seems full of these tensions and competing and contradictory emotions.

~

It's exhausting. And it's horrible to be so lonely in company. It seems 'Other People' are crucial to my well-being, yet simultaneously lead to a diminution of my well-being by failing to transform themselves into Billy.

'Other People', I discover, are a massive part of mourning. They bring both amazing highs and dreadful lows to the situation. They play a huge role in my grieving, and I play a role in theirs. I am of course not the only person who has lost Bill – his friends and family adore and miss him too and are suffering their own grief, and so we all have to accommodate and make room for the randomness and sometimes contradictory nature of each other's needs and feelings, and negotiate our ever-changing responses to each other.

There's that word again – random. It pervades so many of the themes of loss – the randomness of who helps and who doesn't; what behaviour helps, and what doesn't; and how those things can change from day to day, hour to hour, person to person.

Just as most people don't quite know what to do or how to be with me, I similarly don't quite know what is expected of me. In the world of improvisational comedy there's a game whereby one person has to respond to the other's questions. Yet every answer they give is met with an expression that tells them clearly that they have provided the wrong response, and they have to try to work out from the face and body language of the questioner what answer they should have given instead. Like many improv techniques, it can make for very funny, but also very disturbing watching as you see the person squirm with embarrassment and anxiety as they try to change their answer to please their interlocuter. I now feel very much like that person. With all the squirming awkwardness but none of the humour. I feel an obligation to give my well-wishers the responses and behaviour that they want, all without knowing what that is. How much grief is too much? How much is not enough? I feel guilty if denial means I am having a good day and looking as though I am okay and not too badly affected when they were expecting to see me sobbing and in pieces. They had been all geared up, poised and ready to go into sympathy mode and instead are made confused and uncomfortable by seeing me in seemingly good humour, functioning well and cracking jokes. And then I also feel guilty on the bad days when I can't pull things together and instead weep and wail when they don't quite know how to deal with such mess, and were hoping just for a nice little chat where we could all pretend it hadn't happened and marvel at how well I am doing. How am I supposed to know what they are expecting? Am I fulfilling their image of what a grieving widow looks like? Have I deprived them of their chance to comfort, give advice, feel good about how caring they are? Or, alternatively, have I traumatised and terrified them into shocked silence at my inability to cope or manage my feelings? I feel responsible for them, just as they feel responsible for me.

My 'support team' soon learn that there is no single or easy way to be with a grieving person because what I need changes with the wind. And I soon realise there is no single or easy way of coping with my myriad well-wishers and fellow mourners. But one thing does remain fairly constant, a thing I am growing to dread – the question that I hear a hundred times a day, both from my best friends and from people I barely know:

'What can I do?'

It is always said with incredible love, concern and care, but it has become a question that feels so unanswerable that I have reached the point of hating it. Then I hate myself for being so ungrateful. But the truth is that I don't know what they can do. I don't know what I can do. Can anything be done? Is this even a doing thing?

How can I answer these poor, well-meaning well-wishers? What can I ask them to do? What can I tolerate them doing? Such a hard question to answer when at the moment I feel so divorced from myself that I don't really know how to recognise my need for even basic things like food, sleep, going to the loo, getting dressed.

But I'm going to give it a go, if only to save others from having to reach the point of hearing me scream with frustration in response to their kindness.

My personal list – and of course it can only ever be personal, others may feel very differently – is going to start with: stop asking. Just do. And in the early days, in the immediate aftermath, that is going to include something like the following:

- Write a note – as opposed to an email. Something actually coming through the letter box makes a massive difference and gives the grieving person something to physically open and keep. If you don't know their postal address, find someone who does – don't ask the griever for it, they have enough admin to cope with.
- In the note, write down some of your memories of the dead person and say why they were important to you. Tell them how you know the person and where you fit

into their life. Grieving people are hungry for any news at all of their loved one, however minor or out of date. They want to keep them present, in the forefront of everyone's mind. You can help do that through your anecdotes and memories. Let them know you too are impacted by the loss of this massively important person, that it matters to you that they are missing, that their life meant something.

- Tell them who else you have been in touch with so they know who has been told and who hasn't and, if the funeral is imminent, let them know if you are coming or not. Offer to tell others who maybe haven't heard yet.
- Make it clear that you do not need a response. Do not add to their burden of responsibility.
- Make some food – any food – and take it round or have it delivered, but don't offer to share it with them; they may not be hungry or may not feel like seeing anyone.
- Take them a book or a magazine or a playlist or a box set, something to distract them that is not too taxing.
- Take them books about grief – there are lots out there. It may be too early for them to be able to engage, or it may help them to know that what they are feeling is normal, and that others do survive it, and how. I found C.S. Lewis's *A Grief Observed*, *No Death, no Fear* by Thich Nhat Hanh and Decca Aitkenhead's *All at Sea* particularly useful but there are plenty of others.
- If you are there in person, make your own cup of tea, pour your own wine; don't expect the grieving person to act as host as they may feel incapable of movement. But if they want to do it, let them – they may need the

illusion of control or appreciate doing easily manageable distraction activity.

- Do the washing-up, feed the cats, walk the dog, entertain the kids, wipe the table – just use your eyes and see what needs to be done.
- Take a book and offer to sit quietly and not talk but just be there so they don't have to be alone. Offer to spend the night – and change and wash your own sheets if you do so, otherwise bereavement can start to feel like you're running a B and B.
- Maybe take a vase – the quantity of flowers that arrive often far exceeds the number of vases to be found in a normal household.
- If you have a holiday home somewhere or if you live in a different part of the country, or in a different country, offer an invitation to stay whenever they feel the need to escape.
- If you are a very good friend, you are going to have a different role from that of those who are less close. You could offer to help plan the funeral, go with them to register the death, ring whoever needs to be rung to cancel memberships, subscriptions, direct debits, bank accounts.
- Very importantly, tell them you love them. A lot. Tell them you will continue to be there for them in the years to come. They need to hear that they still matter to someone, and they need some measure of reassurance that they are not going to be abandoned further.
- If you have a specialist skill, offer that – a private yoga class, a massage, a haircut.

- If you spot something around the house that you could mend or make better, just do it. My friend Sherie went out and bought nails and a hammer and took it upon herself to mend the long-broken garden fence. The incongruity of it turned that day's tears into laughter, and so cheered me up as well. In fact, I started making jokes about how I could get the whole house redecorated if I went on crying long enough. One has to take what perks one can when one's life has imploded. Sadly, though, no one took me up on that particular request.

As the immediate aftermath turns into weeks and months, a friend's role changes and becomes arguably even more crucial. This is when you are truly needed, when you and others have returned to normal life, but when the spouse realises they have no normal life to return to. What you can do then is:

- Keep ringing, keep texting, keep checking in, keep inviting yourself over, or inviting them out. Keep letting them know they are loved and valuable and that there is a life for them out there, albeit not the one they were hoping for. But make it very easy for them to refuse if they aren't up to it. Don't assume you know what is best for them. You don't.
- Invite them out for a walk, to go to the cinema, to watch telly at your house, to cuddle your dog, to go to the theatre, a football game, a horse ride – whatever it is you know they like to do. But keep it manageable and

untaxing. Don't ask them to big social events where they will have to converse or explain themselves or attempt to be witty or pretend to care about other people.

- If there are specific jobs that you know the partner did – like getting the car serviced or doing all the cooking – then offer to help them do that job so they don't feel swamped by the extra unfamiliar work.
- Allow them to keep talking about the person who has died; don't make them feel they ever need to stop. Keep asking about them, and keep telling your own stories and memories about them. We need to know they haven't been forgotten, that you miss them too, that they mattered and are still alive in the minds of others.

These are just some of the practical things my friends have been doing, all of which I have appreciated – and all the more so when they were just proffered without me having to hear that damn question first.

If I'm being really honest, however, there is one true response that I really want to give to the dreaded 'what can I do' question. It is not an answer anyone actually wants to hear, but it is what I feel I need more than anything. What I truly want to say goes something like this:

What you can do is accept me in all my messiness and unpredictability. You can accept that just because in one moment I seem fine and I'm smiling and having a rational conversation, that doesn't mean I'm coping. It means I'm having a moment of being okay. Or it means that I don't trust either you or myself enough to admit to not being okay because that is too much of a slippery slope towards meltdown and chaos and I need to keep the veneer in place at this precise moment.

Please be aware that this moment of okay-ness could switch at any point. I might suddenly leave the room, or snap at you, or be inexplicably grumpy. What you can do is accept my sudden and spontaneous mood swings, my anger at irrational things, my needing to suddenly stop mid-sentence. Go with the mood swings – pretend I'm a chaotic toddler leaping from feeling to feeling and indulge me in my volatility.

Let me talk. Don't talk at me. Don't tiptoe round me. Don't talk about holidays, or Christmas – those things terrify me. Don't fire questions at me about anything to do with the future. I can guarantee I do not know the answer to anything that involves what lies ahead.

Take your cue from me. Don't be surprised if I suddenly need to change the subject. I may have thought it would be safe discussing X but then a memory pops up and I can no longer discuss X. Please allow my unpredictability. A version of the horrible, sexist old adage, *it is a lady's prerogative to change her mind*, can be applied here – it is a grieving person's prerogative to change their mood. So please accept my sudden need to talk now. Or to shut up now. Or to be busy now. Or to collapse now. To want you around, to not want you around a moment later.

What you can do is not be fooled by the surface presentation. Please accept that because I was all right a minute ago doesn't mean that I can carry on at this pace. I can't; the adrenaline has gone, I've collapsed. Think puppies who run around madly then fall asleep mid-step wherever they land.

Don't say, 'You're doing so well'. I don't know what 'well' means. Does it mean that I'm getting dressed, holding down a conversation, not acting like a two-year-old? By telling me I'm doing well you are in fact assuming that seeming okay means being okay, and it does not acknowledge how awful I am feeling underneath. You are also taking away my option to 'not do well' sometimes. It feels like being told that seeming okay is great and commendable but collapsing and screaming as I really want to do occasionally is not so permissible. And anyway, what is the alternative? I'm just getting on with life in the only way I know how – one foot in front of the other, day to day. Grief has forced me to live in the moment in a way that no amount of meditation can do. I have no choice. The past and the future are too painful to reside in for long. Future plans feel meaningless, past memories painful.

Please don't say anything that you think will make me feel 'better' or cheer me up, or that contradicts what I have just told you. Platitudes such as 'time heals' are really hard to hear – and I say this in the full knowledge that I too have said such things in my time, and that some of my best friends have said this to me; it's only natural. We all do these things with the best intentions, but hearing it minimises Bill and his importance and centrality in my life. Time does not always heal. And right now I do not want to be healed, or cheered up; I want to mourn the love of my life, not think that he is so unimportant that there might be a day when I can brush it off and say I'm over it. In my current state I do not want to be over it, ever.

And time can also make it worse because the gap since I last saw him is longer and he is receding further into the past. The time I have had to keep going, pretending to be okay, is longer, the cumulation of all that effort is taking even more of a toll. And to say I'm getting better suggests that I am suffering from an illness for which there is a cure, rather than having entered a whole new world that I do not like or want but which I am forced into making the best of, and which is my new reality, not a temporary blip.

When I say I miss him, don't tell me I can still talk to him. I KNOW THAT. And I do. Constantly. But guess what? It's not the same. I tell him things, but he doesn't answer. Yes, he's in me and I feel his presence, but I want him outside of me as well, where he can be of some use! In fact, please don't try to reassure me or 'make it better' in any way. I know I can talk to him, and I know he's listening, I know you think it will get better in time, I know he's in a better place, I know he's not suffering, on and on and on it goes, everyone trying to cheer me up. Please don't. You have no idea how little those things help; how trivial they seem in the face of my overwhelm. All that happens when you say those things is that I am then forced to smile, put on a brave face, reassure you that yes, I'm sure you are right, because I don't have the heart to say you have actually just made me feel worse with your lack of under-standing and caused me to feel even more alone as I squash my real feelings even deeper.

Those are some of the things I would like to say but I don't because I know it's the anger talking, and that I have even less clue than you as to what will help and what won't, so how can I possibly blame you for saying all the things that I would probably also be saying if the situation were reversed. And I don't want you to be scared of me or handle me with kid gloves or worry about saying the wrong thing. It's inevitable that you might because none of us, me included, know it's the wrong thing until it happens. As the above list proves, what I want and what I don't want can be contradictory from day to day, so indulge my whims and don't take offence when what cheered me up yesterday causes tears today. It's not about you.

The most baffling thing is that people seem to genuinely think that if they don't talk about Bill then I won't be upset. One friend apologised for 'raking up' a story that had led to me crying, as though I was getting upset all over again rather than just allowing an outlet to something that had been plugged up, that I was making the internal external, which is a good thing, to get it out there. In fact I find the whole 'trying not to upset me' thing quite weird. Do people really think I'm not always upset anyway? That I have forgotten until they mention it? As though I'm okay just because I'm acting okay? Truly, nothing you can say or do can make it worse than it is, because the worst has already happened.

If this all sounds hard – it is because it is. It really is. Being with a bereaved person is the hardest job in the world and I salute every single one of you that makes that effort despite your own fear and misery, despite knowing that you will get it wrong. You cannot fail to get it wrong at times because you are dealing with someone going through a massive, confusing, life-changing trauma who doesn't know what they want or need from one minute to the next. And that is okay; it cannot be otherwise. So maybe the real answer to 'what can I do?' is 'you can be okay about the fact that sometimes you will get it wrong.'

Here's a story that in many ways sums up what I feel about what constitutes good help. I have a friend named Inge, who at the time of Bill's death was unemployed and living in Bristol. She offered to come and stay one Sunday night, very early on. Her own grief for him, and probably some fear about how to best support me, led to her drinking too much on the Saturday night before her arrival. She was coming up from Bristol by bus – a 7 a.m. bus at that. She arrived at my house a few hours later, very emotional, hungover and tired from her early start and long bus ride. She had brought wine and chocolate and popcorn with her. We spent the day chatting, laughing and crying. This was still in the very early days when I couldn't eat or drink, so she ate the chocolate and popcorn and drank the wine herself, getting a bit drunk again. By the end of the night she was distraught:

'Before coming I asked a friend what I should do to help you and she told me to cook, fill the freezer, clean the bath, organise the funeral and wash the floor. Instead I've done nothing but cry and I've eaten all the food and drunk all the wine I brought you. I feel terrible. I'm a useless friend,' she sobbed.

'Inge, I'm not hungry, I rarely clean my bath or wash my floor at the best of times, and I can easily live without those things. What is important to me is that you dropped every-thing, got on a bus at 7 a.m. on a Sunday morning and trav-elled all the way up here with a hangover for several hours just so you could be with me. What I need more than anything is to feel that people love me and are prepared to spend time with me, and share my pain, and that is what you have done. That to me is far more valuable than getting my bath cleaned.'

~

I've found listening to podcasts helpful, and there is one in particular by the Buddhist teacher and psychotherapist Tara Brach that I return to often. One of her stories is of a travelling knight coming across a deserted wasteland devoid of life, in the midst of which he found a castle where a similarly weak old king lay waiting miserably for death. His extensive staff were lavishing expensive food, wine and medicines on him but could not find a way to cure him.

The knight approached the king's bed and asked him 'Where does it hurt?' Hearing this simple expression of care, and the knight's willingness to listen to him tell of his pain, the king came back to health. As he did so the lands around his castle blossomed into flower and colour.

The message of this simple tale echoes what I was trying to convey to Inge, and what I am suggesting you do for your friends – just be there. Show that you care. Just ask, in the general, metaphorical or literal meaning of the phrase – whatever feels appropriate – where does it hurt? Then sit back and be alongside the person as they talk in any way and about anything they like. This 'being alongside' is another good description of what we try to do in therapy. We sit with our clients in their pain. We don't ignore or minimise it, nor do we allow ourselves to be overwhelmed by it, and we don't try to solve it. We don't try to distract from it or get angered by it.

We just be with it and show that we can bear the horror and anger along with them, whatever form that takes.

To return, briefly, to looking at this in attachment theory terms, I think that neuroscientist Louis Cozolino says it best when he says that we should not be talking about survival of the fittest, but survival of the nurtured. Those who feel loved will get through. So nurture your grieving friends as you would a small child. Nothing more complicated than that is needed.

As the December days darken further, I notice my grief changing shape internally and externally. I can feel the cushioning effect of the shock and trauma wearing off – I picture the bubble wrap around me starting to deflate. Beneath it my skin feels raw and bleeding. It's as though it is seeping gunk, weeping what should be internal fluids into the external world. This is a disgusting image, I know, and it's a disgusting feeling. I feel more vulnerable, less protected against those more real, more authentic feelings I've been avoiding. Now they are invading, sensing a crack in the fortifications. I seem to be cycling through many emotions, relentlessly and speedily, with no time to get used to one before the next knocks me off course.

I burst into tears regularly now. I open a drawer and see Bill's stuff – one of his endless lists in his tiny, neat handwriting, or an article cut from a newspaper – things that were once loved and important to him, but which are now useless, mere rubbish. Tears of nostalgia spurt out. So I get myself out of the house. I pass a nice-looking cafe and think how nice a cup of tea and a cake would be, but then I remember he can't come with me. Sobs of self-pity rack my body. I open the weekend

newspaper and throw the sports section straight into the recy-
cling bin unread, and howls of pain stream forth. A letter
addressed to him lands on the doormat and I crumple to the
floor, whimpering. Daily life feels too unbearably sad.

I become immune to crying in public, lose all shame. I walk
down the street with tears pouring down my face, I sit on the
tube snivelling, I lose the power of speech mid-sentence. I
wonder why we ever gave up the tradition of mourners wearing black, or even just a black armband, anything to alert
others to our fragile state. I wonder if I should design a badge,
like the 'Baby on Board' badges that pregnant women wear so
they will be offered a seat on the tube, but instead saying 'Grief
on Board'. I feel similarly incapacitated and unable to act
normally. So I just surrender to it all. I have no choice.

Then comes an even more dramatic meltdown. I attempt a
night out with friends. But everything goes wrong: my wobbly
mood and unfamiliarity with being 'on a night out', the loud-
ness of the venue, the jolliness of those I am meeting, who
happily chat about their lives, which seem to be rolling merrily
along. 'Rational me' knows that however much anyone misses
Bill, their lives are not fundamentally changed by his disappearance; they can, and should, carry on much as they always
have done. 'Grieving me', however, has had her life completely
overturned and loathes that others can continue their lives as
normal. She is furious that these people dare to talk about
other things than him. For her, he is still the only subject of
conversation worth having. I start to hyperventilate. I realise
this must be what a panic attack feels like. In tears I mutter
apologies to the group and stumble out into the London night.

*   *   *

I'm not sure I can survive this. My heart is beating so hard I wonder if I'm now having a heart attack. My legs give out from under me and I sink to the pavement. People step over me, clearly thinking I am a drunken partygoer. Where is my damn 'Grief on Board' badge now that I am in serious need of help? I'm in central London – where I have lived and worked and socialised for thirty years – but now I can't remember how to find the tube or hail a taxi. I feel real terror as my every instinct tells me to throw myself into the road and bring an end to this pain. I remember how I swam out to sea in St Lucia but did eventually manage to persuade myself to turn back to shore. Somewhere in my brain a similar small voice of rationality tells me to grip on to the wall I have slid down for safety, get my phone out and call my friend Louise. Despite my inability to talk properly, she grasps the severity of the situation and tells me to get myself a cab home immediately, and she will meet me there.

I have no memory of getting home, but when I do Louise is there waiting for me, having just upped and walked out of the restaurant she was in. She holds me for the entire evening, and I cling to her physically and metaphorically. Eventually, in her presence, I am able to calm down.

Overwhelmingly strong emotions like this start to permeate all aspects of my life, some recognisable, some less so. But all these intense and conflicting feelings – sadness, terror, anger, confusion, despair – have something in common: what I am experiencing can be summed up, basically, as pain, not so pure and not so simple. It's horrible.

*   *   *

But oh look, here comes 'therapist me' to remind 'whimpering, floundering me' about William Worden's tasks of loss. He named his second task 'process the pain of the loss'. Oh, this feels like a TASK all right, it's bloody hard work being this emotional.

~

I think I prefer Worden's nomenclature of 'tasks' to Kubler Ross's 'stages'. 'Stages', to me, gives the impression of something linear and sequential – something to be passed through and ticked off before progressing to the next. To be fair to her, she never actually said this, and the story has it that it was all the fault of her publishers, who needed neat categories and chapter headings and a sense of progression to help sell the book. But the word itself is somewhat problematic as, for me at least, it does evoke a sense of something with an end goal. Worden's word 'tasks' for me has more of an ongoing sense to it, like the everyday chores that are never truly over but need repeating and repeating – like washing up, commuting to work, putting the bins out – and which just get absorbed into your life on a loop. Are your life. As grief is now my life.

But others may find the word 'tasks' problematic. It may conjure up all sorts of unwelcome connotations. And that is the point with these theories – they will not all speak to all people. Some will like to think in 'stages', some in 'tasks'. Some will like neither and hate all labels or attempts to categorise or neaten this messy process.

There are some universals and common themes, but everyone's grief is as individual as they are. What resonates with one will alienate another. We all have to find our own way through. For some of us that will be wanting the structure of a theory, for others it will be rejecting all theory. Go with whatever works for you. Or pick and choose depending on your daily mood. There is no right way to do this.

One of the other things I personally like about the word 'tasks' is that for me it accurately reflects all the hard work needed to get through this damn grief process. You really do have to engage and work at it if you are not to become a jellied mess merging with the sofa. Not that I don't have those sofa moments too – of course I do, and they are also part of the work – we need to allow the downs as well as the ups, the wallow as well as the denial, as well as the rage or tears. For it can often be in those jellied puddles of collapse that the feelings I've been avoiding with my busyness do find space enough to bubble to the surface, find their outlet. And find the surface they do.

It's time to talk feelings.

Let's begin with that complicated, disturbing and explosive feeling – the one so dominant in Kubler Ross's model that she names it as her second stage – anger.

I've been feeling it a lot, but it is diffused anger, general rage. Unlike some people, I don't really have an obvious focus for it because Bill's death was no one's fault. It wasn't Bill's fault he died – he'd kept himself healthy and fit; it wasn't the doctor's fault – he'd done what he could; no one had knocked Bill down in an accident or punched him in a fight. There is no obvious villain of this piece. Who can I be angry with?

Others have more obvious targets and their anger feels completely justified – against the person responsible for the death, if there is such an obvious anti-hero; or the doctor who couldn't save them; or the system that brought them so low – be that corporate, political, familial. Doreen Lawrence OBE's anger has fuelled her fight for justice for her son Stephen and led to huge transformations in our policing systems. Many others have similarly used their rage to go on to do amazing things.

Until now I haven't had a clear focus, so my more general-ised anger has felt confusing and unjustified. It has been getting misdirected – outwards at people or things that don't deserve it, or inwards to myself and my own failings. I have been berating and hating myself for not having made better decisions at the hospital, for not having said more to Bill at the end, for not having been a more loving wife. I take my anger out on the nearest person because I'm not able to let it out more relevantly – at a supermarket assistant who can't explain why the tomatoes have been packaged in plastic, so has to suffer me blaming her personally for choking the sea life in the oceans, or at my poor mother because she is the safest and easiest person to let rip at, even though she has been nothing other than kind and willing to help. And that's part of the problem: everyone has been so kind, and Bill's death was no one's fault – so where to constructively channel my rage? I find outlets wherever I can and sometimes there are far fewer than six degrees of separation between a rational response and a hysterical one.

For instance, when I had been contacting people to let them know of Bill's death, one friend had not responded to my email asking him to contact me. I felt the length of their friendship merited at least that I tell him personally rather than announcing it in an email or have him find out accidentally. But he never responded, and he didn't come to the funeral. Weeks later he did reply, apologising for the delay and asking me for my phone number so he could ring. He didn't mention Bill, nor his death, so I still didn't know if he had heard the news or not. I sent another email, carefully worded to try to find out what he knew so I could gauge how much I could say. He sent another cryptic reply so, getting more frustrated, I spelled it out for him:

'I've been treading carefully because I need a clue as to whether you have heard what happened?'

'Oh yes,' he replied, 'I did hear . . .' before launching into a long explanation of how busy he had been at work.

I exploded with fury – that nought-to-sixty feeling, taking me from mild irritation that he was thwarting my attempts to tell him nicely – which I felt was more than he deserved anyway – to overwhelming rage. I found myself wanting to scream at him about how he couldn't even be bothered to come to the funeral of one of his oldest friends and was too fucking stupid to realise I'd been tiptoeing round his feelings for a reason. Why did he think I was trying to get hold of him, for fuck's sake? Certainly not for the pleasure of chatting to him. I don't know much about death etiquette but surely one of the more obvious things one should do is realise that it is up to the person who is not the widow to say something to that widow. A mere 'I'm sorry to hear' would have sufficed, or just – 'Yes, I know he's died, thanks for trying to let me know.' Anything, anything, just not a stupid email dance saying nothing and causing me to have to worry about him, just when I needed all my strength to worry about myself, and the people who were genuinely grieving Bill.

I hated that so-called friend. In that moment I genuinely wished him ill. I wanted to hurt him and for him to know that he had betrayed Bill unforgiveably. And in that moment, I genuinely believed he had done so.

That sounds extreme. And it is. The anger inherent in grief is huge and can feel murderous. Of course I'm not really all that angry at clumsy friends, or at the people in the supermarket, or the many other targets at whom I unfairly vent my rage. I'm angry that Bill is gone for no reason, that my life has been ripped out from under me for no reason. In Freudian terms this could be seen as the defence of displacement. This is when you satisfy an impulse for one thing (in my case overwhelming rage at the abstract unfairness of the world that took Bill from me) through a substitute object, in this case any concrete thing or person in my path that feels even mildly unfair.

Society tends to expect, and understand, and forgive, the tears and sadness that come with grief; but it is less comfortable with the anger. It's somehow seen as inappropriate and over the top, and so it can evoke shame in those grieving, followed by attempts to suppress it. But it is not only society that tells us which emotions seem appropriate. We also have our own inner thought police guiding us in one direction or another.

~

When in those moments of really feeling the feelings, when truly 'in' it, there is no rationality, just an outpouring of unmediated responses. In my case, those feelings do often tend to be ones with an angry flavour. Truth be told, from an early age anger has been a horribly familiar response of mine. I might even say it is my 'go-to' emotion, occurring far more often than I would like. And there is a reason for this. To explain it I need to return again to John Bowlby's revolutionary work defining attachment theory, and an aspect of it that he called 'internal working models'.

Attachment theory teaches us that the relationships we experience as infants create the basis for how we structure our image of ourselves, and our place in the world. We start to form rules about how the world works based on what we do and don't see, feel and hear from our caregivers.

Let's look first at how we learn to speak, as it makes for a good analogy for how our internal working models are formed. As infants we learn to speak naturally. Without consciously knowing that we are doing it, we internalise the rules of grammar. No one has to sit down and explain them to us. From listening and experimenting, we absorb rules such as a subject coming before a verb, which comes before a noun, even though we don't yet have names for these parts of speech. From these basic building blocks we slowly grasp, in a similarly subconscious way, how more convoluted sentence structures layer on top. Before we ever hear the words 'subjunctive subclause' or 'conditional past perfect' we are already speaking in complex sentences. Of course, early on a few funny mishaps occur – of the 'me want toy' variety – but generally we manage pretty well, and pretty quickly, to structure a sentence in a way that is meaningful to someone else who knows the same language. We thereby learn how to communicate our thoughts, wants, needs, and so much more.

It is at a similarly early age, and in an equally non-explicit manner, that we learn how relationships work, what is expected of us and how best to please the caregivers on whom we are reliant for validation, love, nurture, and therefore ultimately survival. From this early learning we extrapolate out, believing we understand how all relationships work, what others want from us and how the world works. We tailor our behaviour accordingly, safe in the knowledge that by following these rules we will understand and be understood, and that thereby we will successfully negotiate our way through life.

It is not always quite so easy, however. While language learning tends to be pretty consistent among those who speak the same language, the rules governing relationships tend to be unique to our own families, so misunderstandings with others can abound.

Again, I'm going to start with an example from the world of language to illustrate my point. There is an old joke about the English and the Americans being divided by a common language, but even within certain parts of the British Isles words can mean different things to different people. Chaos, even tragedy, can ensue when this is not realised.

In most of southern England the word 'while' means 'during'. But in parts of northern England 'while' means 'until'. A (hopefully) apocryphal story I once heard involves a sign on a level crossing somewhere in the south of England reading 'Do not cross while lights flashing.' A traveller from the north, seeing this sign, took it to mean that he should not cross UNTIL the lights flashed . . . so he waited for them to do so, then set off across the tracks – just as the train bore down on him.

Variations on this lack of understanding are played out to a greater or lesser extent within most relationships when we don't understand that others might have grown up learning a different emotional lexicon to us.

We assume that what we mean by something is understood in the same way by others, but unfortunately things can be understood in as diametrically opposed a way as in the linguistic example above and can also lead to similarly tragic consequences within our relationships.

For instance, the unspoken 'rule' in some families is to instinctively always try to 'make things nice' and act as if everything is okay, even when it isn't. Acknowledging that something is wrong could be seen as shameful or weak or as upsetting to the other party. So a difficult emotion like anger is not really 'allowed', and any expression of it is frowned upon.

How does the child know this? Does Mum or Dad sit them down at the age of three and explain clearly: 'We only want to believe nice things about others and about the world and we will ignore or deny all evidence to the contrary and if you want us to love you, and keep feeding you, then we would like you to also subscribe to this worldview?'

Well, yes and no. Sometimes it is explicitly stated in all sorts of ways:

'It's not nice to get angry, now is it?'

'Anger is such an ugly emotion, we don't want to see it in this house.'

'Only those with no self-control get angry.'

'People won't want to be friends with you if you are so grumpy all the time.'

'You'll upset little Jimmy if you get angry, and we don't want little Jimmy to get upset now, do we?'

And a hundred other variations along these lines.

But just as often, these things are not so explicitly stated and yet we learn them anyway. And just as with language learning, most infants have unconsciously picked up on these rules long before they are ever verbalised or 'taught'. How? Well, the rules are just as much in evidence in what is transmitted implicitly in a facial expression, a gesture, via body language, an almost imperceptible mood change . . . It may be in the rush to reassure that follows hot on the heels of any glimpse of an unwanted emotion – 'It's all fine, you're okay,'; 'There's nothing to shout about, look how wonderful life is,'; 'Surely you can't be angry with your sibling over something so tiny, they are so much smaller than you, don't you want to be the bigger person?'

There can even be downright denial – 'That is not something to be angry about'/'No one else would find that upsetting'/'What's wrong with you that you are not okay with this?'

Sadly, there are even variations that use mockery – 'Don't be such a drama queen,'; 'Stop making a fuss about nothing.'

The rule may be transmitted via even more insidious ways. It might be that one family member gets to hold all the anger and everyone else must tiptoe round that person. Or you may try your best to be so unlike that angry person as to forbid yourself any characteristics that resemble them, even when anger might be justified.

Just as with language, we absorb what we see and hear and feel around us until this way of being, this way of fitting in with those with whom we are in relationship, imprints on us as an unspoken rule for how we are meant to act in life. Bowlby termed these rules learned within our attachment relationships our 'internal working models'. They constitute the emotional 'grammar' underpinning our way of communicating. It doesn't take long for them to become so ingrained that we don't question them, or even know that we have imbibed them as rules. We just think that's the way the world works – 'everyone knows that' – 'while' means 'during'. But then you meet someone from another 'tribe' who doesn't know your rules and is following their own contradictory ones, those for whom 'while' means 'until'.

Another family may have welcomed expressions of anger, seen it as a show of strength, used it to avoid being sad ('Only weak people cry'/'Only if you're stupidly over-sensitive would you find that upsetting'/'Don't get down, get even.') They may have seen anger as a helpful way of getting what they want because the 'rule' in their family is that saying everything is fine and nice is taken literally, and so you only get someone to take notice of you if you shout and holler loudly.

Another way of responding to the rules is to completely rebel against them. Yet paradoxically, even in reacting in the opposite way from what is acceptable in your family, you are in fact still acknowledging your implicit understanding of the rules. To break them you need to have imbibed what they are and to understand the message you are sending by not following them.

The possibilities for miscommunication are endless. What if someone from the family who smiles through messy emotion comes into contact with someone from the angry family? They may feel very frightened or shocked by the visible anger. Or, if they're a family rule rebel, intrigued and seduced by its transgressiveness. Meanwhile, the person to whom rage is merely a way of getting their point across effectively may not understand the impact they have, so may take at face value the 'I'm fine' message from the other, who then gets resentful ('how could they not know that was inappropriate . . .?') The variations are infinite.

Faithfully following our internal working models can mean that we end up with a vocabulary of emotions that is weighted more heavily towards certain feelings and ways of coping than others. Some emotions we slip into readily, some we avoid. We end up covering those that we have learned are 'unacceptable' with ones that were more acceptable within our families of origin. We can adapt as we mature but I believe that in grief, as in childhood, we are less able to mediate our innate, hard-wired responses. Our filters are less robust and we revert to what comes naturally, take solace in familiar ways of being. I talked earlier about a similar thing happening when I automatically reverted to 'dealer' mode to cope with my shock in the hospital and the immediate aftermath.

So I notice that as my sadness, despair and fear rise in their search for an escape route – all emotions that were not really 'allowed' in my family of origin – I take refuge in what is, for me, an easier-to-bear emotion – anger: my rage at the injustice, my fury at having to acknowledge how much better life would be with Bill still in it, my need to find someone to blame.

But what about those other, less familiar feelings that didn't form part of our internal working model?

Many of us have grown up feeling the deep sense of alienation that comes from understanding that what we are feeling is very different from the prevailing family narrative. We have learned to live with a huge dissonance between the deep emotions we actually felt, and those we learned to wear externally. Which means those emotions have been deeply buried for a very long time.

Such is the power of grief that now for me they come knocking, seeking an outlet, an escape from the vault in which they have been held tight for many years, strictly guarded by the anger. An increasingly loud clamour can be heard from behind the vault door slammed shut many years ago in response to the internal working model to never get upset or show fear. I buried those feelings at an early age, but they don't go away – they never go away, they simply lie in wait, and will eventually find a way of leaking out. Grief isn't the only time they seek escape – there are many ways this can happen – but the powerlessness of grief can be a mighty trigger.

I need to find ways to let my grief have the full range of expression. And to do that in a way that feels safe – choosing to let things out of the vault slowly and carefully and at a time and a place of my choosing. That might stem the tide of insidious escapees making a dash for it when I least expect it and throwing me off balance. Might one key to unlocking the vault safely be lying somewhere in my body?

*   *   *

The moment Bill collapsed, my body went into trauma mode, every muscle and sinew clenched and tightened, shutting out the pain. And now, even as other elements start to thaw – my brain coming back online, my emotions starting to fight through to the surface – still my physical body continues to grip. The effort of that, albeit unconscious, gripping causes an exhaustion beyond belief.

I remember a version of this when my dad died – a huge change in how my body felt, grief embodied. But now it is ten times worse. My body, normally pretty fit and vital, feels heavy and solid – a lead weight I've been saddled with dragging around. All the accustomed joy in movement and exercise that I have experienced for most of my life is long gone and I can barely move. Sleep is similarly elusive. Every night I wake three or four times at least, then struggle to return to sleep, often lying awake for hours. This insomnia is seriously affecting my health. I eventually go to an acupuncturist in the hope that she might help. She sticks pins in me and encourages me to check in with my body, something I have seriously been avoiding doing.

'What do you notice?'

'Fear,' I sob.

'Fear of what?' she asks.

Fear of the bleakness of facing a future without the person who was all that made life enjoyable. Fear of how strong and unrelenting the missing him is, how painful it is. I miss him every moment of every day. I miss him when I wake, when I make a cup of tea, or dinner, for one not two, when I watch telly alone, come back to an empty house alone – you name it, any daily occurrence, however big or small, evokes the pain of missing him, the fear I cannot survive such pain, the fear of what the future holds.

And there is another fear there as well. The fear of losing my grip on sanity. I start to have strange thoughts and delusions including the very weird and seemingly very real notion that Bill never actually existed at all, that he was a figment of my imagination. My terror grows. Am I mad?

Madness also feels very present in the lack of control I am able to exert over all these emerging and cascading thoughts, emotions and behaviours. It's completely disorientating, as though I am being remotely controlled by some unseen sadist who will, on a whim, press the 'cry now' button at the most inappropriate moment, who hurtles me, jolting and jarring, from light to dark, control to chaos, denial to reality. I live like a puppet of someone else's crazed machinations – out of control, floppy, terrified, manipulated, in the dark. It is like when you allow IT support to have access to your computer, and you can see the cursor moving around your screen under someone else's command while you sit helplessly by, not quite understanding what is happening as you watch your folders, your work, your life, being moved by an invisible, unknown force.

The lightning speed with which the remote controller moves me from feeling okay to feeling collapsed adds to the destabilising confusion.

I somehow need to reclaim my brain and my sense of self. I have not just lost Billy, I've lost myself. That's what it feels like. I've lost the biggest part of me, I've lost my future, I've lost my sense of identity, of security, of joy, of being loved. And, right now, I've lost control over my emotions. The instinct to throw things, to break things, to destroy, is enormous. The sadist with the 'cry now' button has pressed it and I have no choice but to respond. Fear, anger, madness, sadness – it's all pouring forth.

Just as in the old saw about twenty words for snow, I feel I am now getting close to having twenty words for crying. I'm developing a vocabulary of tears. The variations seem endless – there is the sobbing, the howling, the guttural groaning, the soft, the leaking, the free-flowing, jolting, gentle, rasping, wailing, squeaking, screeching, grinding agonising soundless, body-racking, the lamenting, weeping, shouting, the bass tones that come from deep in my pelvis, seemingly independently. And then there's the differing after-effects these provoke: the despairing, depressing tears that leave me spent and drained as though I've done ten rounds in the ring with Anthony Joshua; the cleansing, cathartic tears that feel more releasing, leaving me lighter and freer; even the rebellious tears that feel stuck inside, unsure how to escape, yet palpable. I can feel them filling me up inside, bloating my body as though they have created a new internal character, holed up inside me, holding me to ransom.

Sometimes the tears burst out with a childlike stamping of my foot at the injustice of it all. I can feel my inner child howling 'But it's not fair!' And truly it is not, not fair at all. I doubt if death ever feels fair to those left behind, and I would not wish this pain on anyone, but I do find myself wondering 'why us?' Bill was a good person, kind, with so much to offer, and was just reaching a stage in his life when he could ease up a bit and start to enjoy the rewards of years of hard work. Why wasn't he allowed to? And as for me, I selfishly think that whatever I did so wrong – and I still question, daily, what that might have been – surely it can't have been so bad as to deserve this emptiness and loneliness? Bill was literally all I had. Why aren't I allowed a husband? Why aren't I allowed children? Why aren't I allowed a family that actually likes and wants to be with me? Why aren't I allowed just one thing that is mine, that loves me unconditionally? But I don't have any of these things. I couldn't have children. Ancient tensions mean I rarely see my family. My husband is gone, and I want to know why he was taken.

Yet the equally valid, and equally unanswerable, question is 'why not us?'

Why should I be allowed more happiness when I've already had so much? I had a husband I loved, who loved me, and who made me genuinely happy. Maybe I should be grateful that I had a whole fourteen years of joy, filled with a love that many people don't get even a glimpse of. Am I being a spoilt self-pitying brat, counting all the losses rather than focusing on the positives?

The answer is of course that all these things are true: I am extremely lucky to have had Bill, and I am extremely unlucky to have lost him. I am unlucky not to have been able to have children, but I am lucky I had a good job that I loved, and which enabled me to connect deeply with others. I am lucky that I have amazing friends, I am unlucky not to get on better with my family.

It's not fair that I am alone now, but maybe it's not fair that I got to experience love for all those years when many others don't. Maybe our quota of love is rationed over our lifetime, and I got mine in one amazing, concentrated dose. Maybe better that than having him for longer but with a slightly dissatisfied, watered-down, okay-ish version of love.

Who can say? None of this makes any sense. Yet still I seek a reason as to why this happened to us.

But it is because there is no reason. As a line in the musical *Hamilton* says so succinctly:

'Death doesn't discriminate between the sinners and the saints, it takes and it takes and it takes.'

Bill and I are no different from anyone else, no more deserving of longevity or happiness or punishment or justice. It just is what it is. And that's truly the hardest lesson to accept.

Which is why, for now, I'm not quite ready to accept it. Instead I continue to feel buffeted by the waves of overpowering feelings – sadness, fear, powerlessness – none of which come easily to me. They do not form part of my internal working model; they are unfamiliar, and therefore unwelcome. Despite my tears I find myself unconsciously evading sadness, pulling on my defences, slipping into something I am more comfortable with – anger or humour or dissociative busyness – until, as always, the sheer force of them breaks through my carefully constructed defences, and the security team guarding them.

~

It feels like there will be no end to it, ever. And truth be told, actually there isn't an end, although it will change shape. The idea of grief as a path can be upsetting because paths tend to have destinations and with grief there is no destination. It never leaves you. It does not go away, and you do not get through it; you just learn to manage it better and hope that it intrudes less, or at the very least that you might be able to wrestle back some sort of control over when and how to let it through. I prefer the idea that grief never gets smaller, but you do get bigger around it.

Returning to how all this fits in with the grief theories, the strong emotions that assail me right now could be seen as an extrapolation of Kubler Ross's second stage, anger, or as part of Worden's second task, processing the pain. Both have relevance. But we could also not use any labels, and instead just acknowledge that there are feelings, lots of them, and that they are painful, and all too real.

I think that if I were forced to give my own name to this 'stage' or 'task' as I experience it, I would simply call it 'feeling the feelings'. And I would acknowledge the need to experiment with ways of living with, managing and allowing those feelings, however unfamiliar or uncomfortable. And the corollary need to be compassionate with myself as to how difficult that is. I would not include any reference to time, as there is no limit that can be put on this. I would not see it as a stage to get through, or a task to conquer. I would give up expecting it to ever end, although I would hope that it might become less intense and less frequent over time. I would also need to acknowledge that in among it my old friends denial and dissociation still step in from time to time. They sense when I can't cope with any more and they pop up to allow me a night off from the pain occasionally. And that's very welcome relief.

Other feelings I discern in this mix are good old guilt and regret. I can't shake the idea that it was somehow my fault. I can't stop feeling guilty for not having been a better wife. I replay every silly argument, every time I didn't listen properly, every time I made him listen to my moaning. I just want the chance to do it over, and better. I would do anything to get him back. I would make any deal with any power – for good or evil – if I could just see him again. I would do a deal of any magnitude in exchange for any amount of time, however tiny, just to have the chance to say a proper goodbye, a chance to tell him all the things that I loved about him, what a massive influence he has been on my life, how much I can't bear that he is gone.

~

This is bargaining, Kubler Ross's third stage of grief. I am tying myself up in knots trying to work out what I can say or do to reverse time and undo what has happened. My brain cannot compute that this horrendous thing cannot be changed. Reality cannot be accepted; there must be something to be done – I just need to work out what it is. Accepting I have no control, accepting the reality of the situation, does not feel like an option.

For me this phenomenon, as with the other so-called stages, has been present from the beginning. It was far more present in the early days than now, but it hasn't completely gone away. And it's not just in actual deal-brokering – I promise to be a better person and never lose my temper again – it's in the replaying of events already happened, a searching for a different ending that, defying the laws of time and space, feels like it could still materialise:

'If I had rung the ambulance earlier, if he hadn't eaten breakfast, if I'd made him go to yoga more often, if he'd retired from his business, if we'd realised how bad his stress was . . .'

I can't let go. This type of magical thinking, illogical and nonsensical as it is, nevertheless keeps hope alive. The endless rerunning of the events leading up to his death and the moments just afterwards are replayed, both out loud and within my mind, and every time I desperately search for a different outcome. Keeping going with a futile hope that at some point the replaying of the story will result in a different ending. Or I come up with ridiculous, absurd offers:

'If I can just run to the park and back without stopping it will no longer be true. If I just stop eating and get to the right weight, he will come back. If I give away all my possessions to the poor and become a better person we can do things differently . . .'

The variations are endless, but the desire remains the same – if I change something he will come back. I have control. Because surely I can't be as out of control over this life-changing event as I feel. If I acknowledge that I really can do nothing about it, my fragile hold on sanity will evaporate and the world will annihilate me.

Many people go to enormous lengths to prevent accepting the utter helplessness they feel. Sometimes great things result – changes in laws, for instance, or great art. If I think about it, that gorgeous monument to a foreshortened love the Taj Mahal could be read as an act of bargaining – if I can build the most beautiful building in the world to prove and honour my love, can I bring her back?

I felt that if I acknowledged and atoned for and undid all the bad things I'd done in my life, Bill might materialise. I even tried praying that I would be taken, not him, as I was so clearly the one to blame. Bill had done nothing wrong. Ever. He was always kind and loving, it was I who was the miserable old cow, so why was he chosen and not me?

In those early moments of madness, I really would have swum the Channel, or given away all my possessions, or gone to be a nun in a far-flung country, if it would have brought him back.

But that choice is not on offer. This is not something I can 'promise to do better next time'. It is absolutely, irreversibly the end, and my brain does not feel able to accept that.

~

Why do we so often blame ourselves when the fault clearly lies elsewhere or is out of our control? Well, it's precisely because of that lack of control. Acknowledging powerlessness is the most terrifying state to be in, and so we do almost anything we can to avoid contemplating the unpredictability and chaos of the universe. To feel safe we need to believe there is some sort of order to the world. Anything. Any sort of structure or logical explanation, however convoluted, is preferable to acknowledging chaos.

Children know this instinctively, and as adults, as with so many things, when faced with dread and terror and the prospect of an uncontrollable world, we seem to regress to earlier ways of coping.

Ronald Fairbairn, a psychoanalyst working in the 1950s, noticed that children in abusive families often prefer to see themselves as bad, worthy of being beaten, and their parents as right to be doing the beating, than to feel their abuse is unjustified. He termed this phenomenon the moral defence.

A child faced with a violent parent has two choices, subconscious ones. She can acknowledge that her abusive parent is failing her, is possibly even unhinged, and that she doesn't deserve the abuse coming her way. That is one – and clearly the logically correct – option. But to take this reading brings huge repercussions. The parent represents the child's safety, her secure place and space, is the person responsible for feeding, clothing, loving her, keeping her alive. Is all that stands between her and chaos. If this parent is not up to the job, then the world is terrifying, and the child is completely at the mercy of an irrational and unpredictable universe. That way lies madness.

If, however, she chooses to stick with the thought that her parents know what they are doing, are capable of looking after her properly, can keep her from the apocalyptic thought that the world is chaotic and illogical, then the only possible reason the parent has for beating her must be that they know better, have seen something in her that she herself has not, and that she herself is bad, wrong, flawed, in need of correction.

The moral defence tells us it is better to see ourselves as 'bad' in a 'good' world, with hope for change by being better, than it is to acknowledge we are 'good' in a 'bad' world that offers no respite.

I can't help but feel there are some remnants of the moral defence going on within the bargaining of the bereaved. Today, further into my grief journey, I no longer see what happened quite so much as a punishment for my failings; nor do I offer quite such unrealistic bargains as I did in the early days. A measure of reality regarding the fact that Bill isn't going to come back no matter what I do has finally lodged itself in my brain.

But the vestiges of bargaining remain, now manifesting as that guilt and regret. I feel guilt that I am alive and he isn't, when he deserves it more; guilt over all the petty arguments we had, the times when I could have been nicer to him, more understanding. Regret that I didn't buy him more presents, make him more breakfasts in bed, laugh more loudly at his jokes. I'm trying to rewrite history. I'm punishing myself for my earlier complacency, for not recognising what I had while I had it.

And that leads to other thoughts: If I'm more grateful for what I do have, if I'm a nicer person to more people, will that somehow redress something? I try to be more giving, generous, understanding and empathic towards my friends (which is not actually very hard as they have all spent the last few weeks being completely amazing towards me); I push the boat out further and volunteer to teach yoga at a local refugee centre, attempting to atone for years of selfishness; I make efforts to be nicer and more understanding to the people who annoy me, to smile more at strangers, give more money to the homeless people I pass on the streets, and to the charity email requests I get. And all this does bring a modicum of pleasure, knowing that I can grow from this experience, find the good in people, give back a bit – be 'more Bill', in fact, pick up his baton in terms of disseminating a little of the love and pleasure he brought to others.

But am I still me? I feel I am trying identities on for size. Does my therapist identity still exist? Is it time to find out?

* * *

I am very aware that my clients are waiting to hear from me. They were told my leave of absence would be indefinite, but it has gone on a long time now and that doesn't feel fair. I arrange a session with my supervisor to talk about how I am, to discuss when might be a good time to return to work.

'Don't go back,' she says. 'What's the rush? You've been through a massive trauma and need time to process it. Take as much time as you need.'

A huge weight lifts from my shoulders and I breathe a sigh of relief. I hadn't known how scared I was about returning to work until I heard her say this. Her words feel like I am being given permission not to resume my practice just yet. I feel so shaky, so unlike myself. How can I help anyone else when I am such a mess? It doesn't feel fair – either to me or to my clients – to offer myself to them in such a fragile state. But I need to let them know not to wait for me any longer if I am not going to be coming back in the foreseeable future. I also feel very uncomfortable about the fact that we never properly finished our work together, that I abandoned them so suddenly. It is terribly bad practice on a professional level but, more importantly, on a personal level it is not sitting right with me at all. I care for these people, I was a big part of their lives, some of them for many years, and I can't just drop them with no further word.

I decide that in a couple of months' time I will offer them the chance to come for two closing sessions so we can talk about how they felt about my sudden departure, review our work up to that point and say a proper goodbye. This feels necessary both for them and me, but while this feels like the right decision, it also brutally highlights how I really don't know who I am any more, or even how I am to earn my living from now on when I'm so broken and incapable. Without Bill I am a mere shadow of my former self. How can I go about un-entwining those melded tree trunks that we had become? It's like filling out that damn St Lucian immigration form all over again, feeling the utter impossibility of picking either 'married' or 'single'. I am neither. I am both. I am lost.

~

Questioning who you are and what you are 'for', in the face of a life that has revealed itself as inherently meaningless, is a state of being that hits many of us from time to time. It's a very frightening experience. Often known as existential angst, it tends to strike at times of challenge or change, often after our sense of security has taken a big hit; so the death of a loved one is obviously a prime contender as a trigger. The knowledge of just how alone and helpless we are in this world is something dwelt upon by a branch of philosophy known as existentialism. Big names in the existentialist world include Kierkegaard, Heidegger, Nietzsche and Sartre, all of whom consider that no one is 'in charge' and the only certainty is death, and so ponder the 'nothingness' of life.

This philosophy has given its name to a similarly oriented branch of psychotherapeutic theory, also called existentialism.

As with existentialism-as-philosophy, existentialism in the therapeutic world is complex, multifaceted and riven with sometimes slightly contradictory beliefs. In its most basic form, existential psychotherapy tends to look at our ways of being in the world, our actual lived experience. It prioritises our own sense of responsibility and purpose given that, in Nietzsche's words, 'God is dead', so we cannot rely on a higher power to offer guidance. The belief is that we cannot understand what causes distress in a person if we don't contextualise, and if we ignore the most basic cause of unhappiness – which is that life feels inherently pointless if you don't know your purpose in it and if there is no belief in a 'higher power' to guide you.

Certainly for me, the purposeful foundation on which I had built my life has disintegrated. I have nothing with which to replace it, and nothing certain ahead of me other than death, an escape route that feels hideously far away. It definitely doesn't feel as though anyone is in control of this crazed world of grief. It is too anarchic and unstructured and, as I have said many times, like being lost in a frenzied ocean in the dark. That so many defenceless children who feel in similar peril resort to the moral defence – blaming themselves for the violence perpetrated against them – shows how far we will go to find a way of making sense of ungoverned chaos.

When I sat on that St Lucian beach sobbing and raging about my inability to understand anything of the incomprehensible planet of grief I'd been flung onto, I had felt the rising presence of my therapist self. I think I was summoning her as my higher power, as someone who might know how to chart a route through the chaos. Her attempts to engage the analytic thinking, history and knowledge of psychotherapeutic theory could be read as my way of searching out structure, or seeking to uncover the grammar underpinning this impenetrable language of loss in which I found myself a foreigner.

Now that therapist self is wondering whether, at this time, the existential approach might constitute another route through. Could existentialism offer another language with which to translate the gobbledegook into something I can understand? And do that by helping me find meaning and purpose to replace what I have lost?

I think this could help me with my current flailing about, could constitute another plank of detritus to bolster the tiny raft I'm building. But as I am discovering, finding meaning is hard! I need to go back to the books. How have those in far worse situations than me managed it?

Viktor Frankl was a psychoanalyst who spent three horrific years in Nazi concentration camps during World War Two. His experiences there gave birth to his own branch of existential psychotherapy, which he called logotherapy. Logotherapy tells us, among other things, that the search to find meaning is a primary motivational force and that the appropriate question to ask is not 'What does life hold for me?' but 'What does life ask of me?' He further suggests asking your client or yourself 'Why do you not commit suicide?', seeing in this deep reflection a way of unearthing your deeper meaning. This was the very question I had asked myself when pondering that option in St Lucia as I swam too far from shore. In that moment the answer I reached was that I needed to not betray Bill's memory, and not upset my friends. Those things were enough to drive me back to the beach that day. Now I can see that those are quite negative reasons – not wanting to upset others – as opposed to more positive reasons. I need to find a less passive and more proactive purpose. I need to do as the existentialists ask – delve deeper into questions of what life asks of me, what my purpose is and how I make sense of what feels, at the moment, very much like senseless suffering.

Frankl believes meaning can be found in one of three ways. Either through what we do, by what or who we meet, or by how we experience suffering. He also believes that meaning is unique to each individual, and to each moment, and can therefore only be found from within; it cannot be imposed by another. To quote Nietzsche once more, as Frankl was fond of doing, 'He who has a *why* to live can bear with almost any *how*'.

This is something I need to find. To help me bear my currently very difficult 'how', living without Bill, I need to find my 'why'.

Yet right now it seems easier to think about all the things I'm not – I'm not a wife, or mother, or therapist. I'm not my old self in any shape or form. Even at the most basic level I feel like I've lost any connection with my former self, starting from the moment I open my eyes each morning. As one of nature's 'larks', throughout my whole life I've been used to waking early with a surge of excitement and energy about what the day might hold. I've always leapt out of bed eager and enthusiastic to get on with my day, starting with some sort of exercise or even just going out into the garden and pootling around there, feeling busy and useful.

Now I wake with a *Groundhog Day*-esque sense of dread, as it is in those moments of regaining consciousness that I have to re-remember all over again that Bill has gone, that I am alone, that I now have to try to drag myself through another day. A day without meaning.

When I think back to the eulogy I wrote for Bill in which I described how we had gone on safaris, climbed volcanoes, stridden out across the globe, I marvel at how the Sasha leaping into those adventures has been replaced by a terrified mouse, scared of everything – her inner world just as much as the outer world. Here now is an unrecognisable person who is scared of visiting the supermarket or having to engage in conversation with her neighbour.

Most terrifying of all is that hideous unknown land – The Future. I cannot even look beyond the next five minutes without panicking.

And yet with Christmas around the corner I do need to make some sort of plan. I ponder my options. All of them seem hideous.

I seem to be depressed.

~

Aha, seems we are on to Kubler Ross's stage four – depression. Again, I want to give a caveat – depression may or may not be part of your grieving process, and even if it is, it may not come to you at the 'right' point in time. For me, it has been very much part of my process, and as with the previous 'stages' I have found myself going in and out of it almost from the word go, found it alternating with the other relentlessly recurring phenomena – denial, pain, emotions, bargaining.

But now, as I contemplate Christmas and New Year, depression makes an appearance big time.

Sadly, it is not an unfamiliar feeling. This is not my first rodeo when it comes to depression. In fact, I have suffered from it on and off my whole life. It began in childhood, was particularly prevalent and intense in my teenage and university years, and then made less frequent and slightly easier-to-cope-with reappearances throughout my twenties and thirties. It appeared to have gone into abeyance from my mid-thirties onwards, from about the time I met Bill in fact, which is probably not entirely coincidental. But it came back with a vengeance after my father died, a horrible time that also coincided with my having to finally accept my childlessness, and the onset of perimenopause. Who knows which of these variables was the primary motivator for its reappearance, or whether it was simply the combination of this wonderful cocktail of life events that opened the door to its comeback. Whatever the cause, or causes, I again began to plummet.

It is really hard to describe depression to someone who has never had it. Bill hadn't, and was endlessly curious about what this thing was that would temporarily cause such a massive personality change in his usually quite upbeat wife. I struggled to explain. Sometimes I would describe it to him in cycling terms, a hobby we both loved; I used to say that depression for me felt like cycling uphill, into the wind, on flat tyres. You put the same amount of effort in as normal, but you don't seem to be getting anywhere and all you can manage is to keep your eyes fixed to the tarmac and dig in, feeling nothing but pain for no noticeable gain. To make any sort of progress requires seemingly superhuman reserves of strength just to keep the wheels turning in place. You wonder why you bother when everything feels so hard for so little reward.

Not being depressed feels like it does when your bike has nicely pumped-up tyres that carry you along beneath a cloudless sky. You still have to work at keeping the wheels turning, especially up the hills, and that isn't always easy. But as you do finally crest each hill you can't think of anything nicer – you're speeding through life, wondering what all the fuss had been about and able to appreciate the beautiful scenery and the feeling of joy and lightness in your whole body.

Which brings me back to now, deeply depressed at the prospect of Christmas without Bill. We had always tended to go away for Christmas but had, unusually, decided that this year, because of having planned the St Lucian escapade for early December, we would stay home with the cats, eat chocolate and binge-watch Netflix. Now, with 50 per cent of the human contingent for that party no longer available, the prospect feels decidedly tragic, however much I love my cats.

My sister-in-law and many of my lovely friends all offer to have me, but the thought of gatecrashing someone else's happy family Christmas – a thing that fate has denied me ever having – would probably finish me off. My mother always spends Christmas with my sister, with whom I don't get on, so that is never an option. I have cousins I could ask to have me, but I won't because, like my friends, they have their own families who deserve to have a happy, child-focused day of tradition. A tradition that doesn't include a grieving add-on.

I feel completely helpless, terrified and panicked by how to get through the Christmas period. I eventually come up with a plan to spend four days volunteering at the homeless charity Crisis. I think it will do me good to work with those in even worse situations than myself.

Turns out it doesn't. I feel worse. I weep and sink lower. I do manage to break up the awfulness by dropping in for a quick Christmas Day lunch with some wonderful friends who live near the Crisis venue; this, despite my misgivings, turns out to provide very welcome short-term relief from the misery. These friends and their gorgeous, wise, sympathetic children are kind and do an amazing job of being okay with this weird, depressive, snivelling wreck sobbing into her sprouts. But overall it is a very grim few days.

Eventually, it is over. Another hurdle hurdled. Another landmark date ticked off.

~

But, God, this is relentless. Now I get to contemplate New Year's Eve. This new horror I broach by deciding to go through with the three-day yoga retreat in Somerset that, like the St Lucian holiday, was booked many months ago for the two of us. Again the prospect of undertaking alone a trip planned for both of us horrifies me but what other choice do I really have? Stay at home on my own and cry in front of the telly? Spend it with friends who will be happy and joyful and excited for the year to come? Both options feel unbearable. The yoga retreat seems like the least bad option. I wonder as I drive there why there is no law against bereavement-driving like there is against drunk-driving. I feel similarly out of control and my vision is impaired by tears. What a mess I am. I can't face people, so on arrival I go straight to bed, at 5 p.m., without supper.

In the morning I flop my way unenthusiastically through a yoga class. I am not really present. I don't feel I can miss any more meals, so I take my place at the breakfast table. But I realise the impossibility of sociability, especially with strangers. For the last few weeks I've surrounded myself with my most trusted friends, to whom I don't have to explain anything. Now I can't seem to hold a conversation. People are asking what I did for Christmas, where I live, what I do – all the questions I need to avoid because they might provoke tears, or require an explanation of my sorry situation. I can't listen to others chatting because they occasionally mention their children or husbands or planned holidays. I hear two women saying how relieved they are to have a night away on their own because their children are so demanding and ever-present. I have the exact opposite problem. I long for a night not on my own, a night with Billy. The real Billy, not the inside-of-my-head-Billy to whom I speak constantly. I note my correct use of whom, and my inability to end the sentence with the hanging proposition 'to' because I know, grammar nut that Bill was, that he would have picked me up on it if I had. Even without him here to correct me I still write, say, do, everything as though he is watching, find myself trying to act in a way that I know would please, or amuse, or comfort him. He is always with me still.

The evening class brings with it a New Year's Eve ritual in which we let go of the old year. The very words 'let go' cause rising panic. How can I let go of the last year in which Bill ever existed? How can I let go of a past that feels like it was, and always will be, the best part of my entire life? No, I want to hang on to it tightly. How can I move into a new year that Bill will never experience? A year in which we will never get to do the things we planned to do in it, let alone the plans we had for the decades ahead. I just don't understand how other people can be getting on with their lives, have hope and plans and things they want to do and things to be excited by and to look forward to, when I cannot imagine a future without Bill in it.

I can't look ahead. I can't look behind. I am trapped in a horrific, agonising present. A present that now involves me being asked to set an intention for the yoga class. A what? What on earth could that mean? I've done this a hundred times in a hundred different yoga classes. We are meant to pick something we feel we need to work on – like kindness, or acceptance, or love for someone who needs it – and to focus on that throughout the practice. But now the words bemuse and confuse me. What could I possibly intend other than to survive the next minute? I can't say I want to get better because I don't. What does better even mean? That I don't feel so much pain? That I forget? That Bill pales in importance? I don't want any of those things to happen. But do I want to stay in this agony? No. I don't want that either. I don't want anything but to have Bill back and that is not going to happen, so I am left flummoxed by the very notion of 'wanting'. I don't 'want' anything. I don't 'intend' anything. I can't let anything go and I can't allow anything new in. All I can do is focus on getting through the next few minutes and hours.

The midnight hour approaches. They want me to dance the new year in. Dance? Be happy? Be joyful? No. Impossible. I can't be joyful. But I can't stay in sadness either. I am stymied. Paralysed. Can't want things to get better, can't stay where I am. Life has just become an endurance test to be got through. None of it's going to be enjoyable, none of it matters. I can't get worked up about Brexit, or austerity, or refugees – I no longer care if Britain goes down the pan, or the oceans warm up. The worst thing in the world has already happened to me, so why should I care if things in the wider world are a little bit worse or a little bit better? Doesn't make any difference. I will still just have to keep my head down and plod on through. Whether through sunshine or rain, it makes no odds.

~

Having the whole 'New Year, New You' greeting-card platitudes forced upon me – however kindly – is too painful for me to contemplate right in that moment, but I can recognise that it is probably an idea that is not without merit in the longer term. It's probably even a useful – necessary – message to take on board, in time and when ready. But no one should ever force any theory, or any platitudes for that matter, on anyone, no matter how much you think it might help the person. You cannot ever know what another person needs. Coming to it in time on one's own is another matter entirely. And knowing other options and ways of thinking are out there can be helpful.

Below is a description of another, more modern grief theory that may be helpful now; or you may want to save it for later; or you may never find it useful. If you are, understandably, getting bored with me endlessly talking about the uniqueness of grief to each person, then I am glad, because that means the message is hitting home – that there is no right or wrong way to get through this; that you need to find what works for you, and allow yourself to do it your way.

The dual process model of grief grew out of the work of two theorists – Margaret Stroebe and Henk Schut – writing in the late 1990s. They felt there were several things missing from traditional grief theories that needed addressing. Firstly they felt that the idea that grief must always be tackled head on was mistaken. This traditional idea – which originated with Freud and was then taken as gospel by many others – was that 'grief work', the facing down of your pain and fears, was the only way to ever get through it, and that without this one could live for ever in denial, with deleterious consequences to one's mental and physical health.

Stroebe and Schut felt this was too confronting. They acknowledged that there is a place for that confrontation with reality and that it is necessary over time and when feeling resilient enough, but they felt that there was also a place for ignoring it and allowing oneself time to pretend, for a while, that it hadn't happened. Going out and enjoying life for a few minutes of gratefully accepted denial was okay, and it didn't necessarily mean that you were suppressing or avoiding anything. Instead they saw it as necessary for pacing one's emotions and taking much-needed breaks from them. Certainly for me that is what happened naturally; I had been feeling, almost from the outset, that I was living two parallel lives and moving in and out of reality and fantasy, whether I wanted to or not. Sometimes choosing when to inhabit either universe was within my conscious control, sometimes it wasn't. And when it wasn't, I believe it was my unconscious taking over, handing me only as much as I could cope with at any one time, before allowing a grateful retreat into forgetfulness or denial when it all got too much. I did not experience this as suppression, more as part of a dynamic relationship with grief – my new companion; a tricky companion whom I need to get to know in small doses rather than in a full-frontal assault.

The second important aspect of the dual process model is the recognition that the pain, fear, anxiety – which they group under the umbrella term 'stressors' – that a grieving person experiences come in two distinct forms, one that looks behind and one that looks forward.

'Loss-oriented stressors' are those that come from engaging with what you have lost – the memories, the communication with the dead person, the yearning. For me this can be activated by anything from walking past a cafe we used to love, to getting an email about a play or film coming up that Bill had always wanted to see, to listening to a piece of music, to hearing someone order a craft beer rather than wine in a restaurant, as he always did. The painful memories of how much I miss him and how much has changed in my life are myriad and endless – they feel like death by a thousand paper cuts, these daily reminders.

On the other hand the 'restoration-oriented stressors' come more from contemplating what lies ahead and coping with how different your life has become – like my tears at unloading the dishwasher because it brought home in just how many hundreds of activities, big and small, I was now alone, how huge my isolation was to be – and how unclear you are about what your new life will look like – for me, what job I could do, how to live my life as a solitary person, no longer part of a couple, what the future might hold practically, financially, emotionally.

*   *   *

Essentially, dual process theory recognises the pull between the past-focused pain and the future-focused pain and, crucially, it acknowledges the dynamic movement between the two – which the theory refers to as oscillation. Also crucially, it allows for and 'gives permission' to occasionally linger in the still point between these two sets of stressors, the place where self-care and the avoidance of either is allowed to lie. And that still point can be whatever self-care means for you – be that under a duvet on the sofa watching Netflix and mainlining chocolates, or being out in a pub laughing and joking with friends, or running it out on a treadmill or dance floor. It can be any one of a million activities, or non-activities, that allow you just to be yourself, not weighed down by the baggage of being a grieving person, but just to be you again, for a few precious minutes.

But I'm still not sure what 'being me again' might look like now. Is there space for a newer version of me to develop – one who might be more able to tackle this New Year that I can't avoid? And where are the more traditional grief therapies in all this? Where has William Worden gone? He's gone to task three, 'adjust to life without him'. Wonder how that's going to work out?

Chapter Four

Floating

I'm going to tackle January and Worden's third task at the same time. Let's acknowledge that I have somehow passed several major milestones, and look at what has already shifted, and at what might be able to start shifting now this unwelcome new year has dawned. Can I do as Worden exhorts and adjust to life without the love of my life? Do I have a choice?

Let's start small and specific. Right now I feel sad because I have reached the end of the last bottle of aftershave Bill bought – I've been wearing it myself to keep him close. Just like I've been sleeping in his T-shirts and boxer shorts, and drowning my increasing bulk in his jumpers. I look ridiculous, of course – I am a five-foot, size eight woman, while he was a six-foot, extra-large-sized man, but I want to give his things the longer shelf life denied him. I even wear his socks, which are also too big and therefore give me blisters. A physical pain that for a few precious moments takes my mind off the emotional pain.

Of course it's irrational to wear his clothes, especially as at best they make me look stupid and at worst they hurt me, just as it is irrational to feel upset by running out of aftershave that doesn't even smell right on me. Of course I could buy another bottle, but that's completely not the point – the actual

169

smell is only a fraction of its appeal, it's the fact that this was an object he had bought himself, that he had held in his hand, that existed in a time before either of us had any clue about what lay ahead. It's something that forms part of the fabric of our shared home, back when his things had their rightful place alongside my own and held no stupid, magical, terrible significance.

I throw the empty aftershave bottle away, reluctantly, as I did the last bottle of shampoo he bought, the last tin of beans, the last bottle of beer, all the tiny remnants of our shared life. Yes, we bought all the furniture together, the art on the walls, the cats even – all of which are still going strong and providing constant reminders that this house was once a joint enterprise. But in the tiny everyday, irrelevant, non-important things like toiletries, Bill is slowly being removed from existence. He is fading away. Not in my brain or heart where it matters, but in matter itself, where it shouldn't affect me, yet does. Death by a thousand cuts, a slow drip, drip of departure and evaporation.

The oscillation as described by the dual process method has been exhausting, the constant switching between those two sets of stressors, the backward-looking pain of what I miss and the forward-looking pain of what I am frightened of. The still points in between those pendulum swings have been few and far between. But now feels like a good time to start trying to engage a bit more with the present moment, the now of the present day. At home that means throwing away aftershave, but outside the home I'm also inching my way forwards, towards the possibility of being a bit more sociable. I've got through my first holiday alone, the first Christmas, the first

New Year. There is even a tiny glimpse of the clichéd new shoots of spring making an appearance in my garden.

So what might my own personal 'new shoots' look like? And what's the weather like over in that hostile metaphorical ocean in which I was last seen thrashing about? When I last checked in, the full force of the tsunami's fury had receded a little and the slightly calmer seas meant I was occasionally able to float, head above water, able to breathe air and scan the horizon. I can't say that I have yet spotted land, but I do spy some flotsam and jetsam bobbing about nearby that might prove useful. Despite my exhaustion I think I have just enough energy to flap my way over there and to grab on. They are only tiny pieces of jagged wood, but together they form the beginnings of a raft and constitute the first solid things I've held on to for months.

This tiny glimmer of hope, like the daffodil shoots fighting through the snowline in my garden, provides a modicum of relief from the panicked flailing of the last few months. Clinging to these metaphorical pieces of wood brings tiny moments of respite when I can relax into some, albeit rather fragile, support.

In real terms those bits of wood represent finding more buoyancy emotionally – I am developing the ability to get through the day without too much crying – and also practically, in that I am developing the ability to be a bit more, well, practical. Being able to throw away toiletries and re-engage with my home (allow it to be a home even) feels quite an adjustment. But the biggest, most important pieces of flotsam and jetsam are my friends. Those stalwarts who have confounded all my fears of being abandoned once the funeral was over, and instead are still here phoning me, calling round, letting me be me in all my messiness. Their attendance means that those still points between the oscillations can even sometimes be quite fun – we go out for nice meals, we go to the cinema, we go to the theatre, we go for walks. We even laugh. I can finally find moments of pleasure and enjoyment and respite from the horror. I love being with my friends and being able to be more active and outgoing again. I feel safe with them; but strangers are another thing altogether. The thought of meeting new people still frightens and triggers me. But now I am confronted with a dilemma that feels very much like a task when I realise I need to pay back some of my friends' love for me by showing some to them.

I'm invited to celebrate my friend Sarah's fiftieth birthday at a ceilidh in the Peak District. Well, she's celebrating, and I do desperately want to celebrate with her, but that sadist has grabbed the remote control again at the prospect, and I can feel a panic rise within me. I've got used to so many new things, and when with that loyal bunch of friends who have been with me since the beginning, I've been able to relax and enjoy their company. But going to a party? Meeting new people? That feels like a whole new ball game – like moving from nursery school to big school.

I'm on the train headed north. At my side I have my suitcase containing my make-up and party dress and shoes, but I'm wearing yoga clothes because I've come straight from a yoga class and thought I would just change properly on arrival. I suddenly realise I have not packed a bra. And I'm going to a ceilidh. If you've read thus far then you will have long ago realised that I do love a metaphor. But I'm going to hold back from following through on the thoughts going through my brain now about having the 'cosmetic surface' props yet lacking the 'foundational support' while being forced to 'dance with others'. You can make up your own metaphors for this current scenario.

Inability to remember to pack a bra aside, I contemplate the other potential perils ahead. I don't really remember how to make small talk. What am I going to say to people? I can't lead with: 'So, my husband just died and I'm in the depths of despair, what have you been up to lately?'

As an opening gambit that's going to put a bit of a dampener on an evening and cause people to give me a very wide berth indeed. But how can I not mention it? It's still the only thing I think about, or talk about, and if I don't mention it, I have nothing else to say. Nothing. This is not the first social occasion I've had to deal with, but for some reason it feels the hardest; maybe because it's out of London and so out of my comfort zone, maybe because I so want my friend to have a lovely birthday and I feel the pressure to 'perform' for her; or maybe it's just one of those periodic waves of emotion peaking, over which I have no control. So, I look for ways to cope; ways that I might be able to find some control. One way is to arrive at the party early to take my mind off the rising panic within and to help Sarah set up. I am delighted to be busy and have a job to do and spend many happy minutes arranging and rearranging the bottles of wine and beer on the counters and putting the glasses into size order. Creating order, seizing control. Hmm, again with the metaphors that I no longer need to spell out to you.

Guests start to arrive and I – to slightly misquote T. S. Eliot – prepare a face to meet the faces that I meet. I've noticed a thing my cats do. If I stroke their backs when they are in a certain position, they will automatically round up to meet my hand. Even if they're in the middle of eating, it feels like they just can't stop their bodies responding and rising to the contact. I sometimes feel a bit like them – as though contact with people draws me unwittingly into a different place. Almost despite myself, as though activated by an invisible puppeteer, I feel myself rise to meet the connection, switch into performance mode. And I do so now. I engage and smile and chat nicely. But soon the performance becomes too much to bear and I sink. Small talk stalls and paralysis steps in. Pretty soon I see my latest interlocutor's eyes darting about as they try to think how to keep this non-existent conversation going; or perhaps they're hoping they might spot someone else they can palm me off onto. It's amazing how many people seem to desperately need the loo, or a new drink, after five minutes with me.

I give up on conversation and throw myself into the ceilidh, thinking movement will help. But I somehow find myself holding hands with a small child to one side of me, and on the other an elderly gentleman who had to put down his walking stick before joining the circle. Neither can hear or understand the caller's instructions, and neither have any sort of coordination or stability on their feet. We crash into each other with every step. This is not dancing, it's dodgems. Here I go again, but how symbolic that line feels – not just of this party, but of my entire life right now: how others are trying hard to get it right but end up stepping on my foot; how out of step the rest of the world is with me right now, and I with them. I'm enduring dodgems, rollercoasters, a ghost train – and bra-less. All the non-fun of this fair.

I abandon dancing and attempt conversation again. But every subject is fraught with pitfalls. One woman asks what I do. I tell her I'm writing a book. She asks what my book is about. I say that my husband died last year, and I don't feel ready to return to work, and that that is what my book is about. The response comes, as they nearly all do: 'Oh my God, oh that's so terrible, oh my God, I'm so sorry I asked, you don't need to talk about it, I'm so sorry.'

I have no idea how to avoid the panic and guilt and terror that I evoke in other people. I could lie and say my therapy practice is going well but a) well, that's a lie, and b) I can say no more as otherwise I'm compounding the lie and creating a complete fantasy, and what is the point of even talking to someone if I'm just making up stories about myself? Stories that at some point they will realise are not true and so they'll be cross with me, and uncomprehending.

I could avoid the question, not answer and just ask them a question about themselves instead, but that a) only shuts them up for a while and b) can get pretty boring for me just listening to others talking about themselves all night, especially when they are full of tales of their happy families and full lives, each of which lands like a dart to the heart.

I give the truth a try: 'My husband has died and I am trying out new ways of being and coping with my life.'

But now I've pretty much ruined their evening for them because they feel horrified that they've 'upset me', they don't know what to say, and I don't know how to reassure them. It's lose, lose. If I say 'It's fine, don't worry, I'm okay' then that's very dismissive and also a lie of sorts, albeit less of a lie than the first option, as it is sort of true at times as well. But I feel disloyal to Bill brushing it off so lightly.

Standing in high heels and a tight dress with a ceilidh band playing loudly and people laughing all around me does not feel like the right environment in which to announce the real truth – that my life has been devastated, I am having to relearn everything I thought I knew and rewrite my whole future. So my poor converser, waiting for me to grapple for something that is not quite a lie but not quite the truth, generally ends up either walking away and leaving me standing, or they try to talk more about it, which I don't really want to do, or they change the subject, which is probably the best option but nevertheless seems to annoy me as well. They really can't win. And neither can I. Tonight's version of this, the follow-up to the customary 'Oh my God, I'm so sorry' exclamations already mentioned, went something like this:

'But you're writing a book, how wonderful, good for you. I always wanted to write a book. I think I've had quite an interesting life, I've always thought I should write about it. How do you go about getting an agent . . .?'

At which point despair overwhelms me and it is I who has to walk off and try again with someone else. Or, eventually, to go and have an intense conversation with the cheese at the buffet table, which asks no questions and soothes me rather marvellously – at least up to the point four hours later when it wakes me in the middle of the night with appalling indigestion that can only be alleviated by spending the rest of the night propped up on pillows and mainlining Rennies.

~

Spring is here and the outside world is gaining more colour. My internal weather report is similarly slowly thawing and being coloured in, albeit only in pastels and with a more limited palette than that I see around me.

If I am not to remain stuck in the past then I do need to properly address my life not just outside of home, but also at home. I cannot keep it as a shrine to Bill for ever. Throwing away a few toiletries now and then is not really going to cut it long-term, so I contemplate whether there are proper changes I can make. I study my overstuffed wardrobe and realise how much easier life would be with more space.

As with any modern couple, particularly those living in tightly packed cities, there was always a battle over space, particularly in the wardrobe arena. I felt that being a woman, and one with an extensive shoe collection and a love of clothes, I should have the room to keep those clothes nicely. After all, wasn't it in his interest if I wore smart things and looked after myself rather than just resorting to jeans and a jumper every day? The fact that 90 per cent of the time I did, in fact, resort to jeans and a jumper – albeit through sheer laziness as opposed to lack of wardrobe volume – didn't distract from the idea that some future me was somehow going to magically transform into the sort of person with the time and energy available to spend time choosing a new, exciting outfit every day. Bill's argument was that, being bigger, his clothes took up more space, and he had to have suits and shirts for work that couldn't be crushed and squished if he was to look vaguely presentable. Stalemate.

This morning, as I wrestle with the usual fallout of stuff from the over-packed wardrobe unleashed by my trying to cram in yesterday's shoes and haul out today's boots, it occurs to me that I could finally have all the space I wanted if I were to get rid of Bill's clothes and allow mine to spread into his wardrobe.

This thought is followed, within a millisecond, by a cascade of other emotions – guilt, grief, pain, confusion and betrayal. For every one step forward I take two back. For every task completed, another five reveal themselves. How can I possibly be contemplating getting rid of more of his stuff? How could his wardrobe become mine? That would suggest there was no 'his' any more. On one level, of course, there isn't; on another, there will never not be. The wardrobe itself is irrelevant but representative of how present he both is and isn't. It sparks the ever-present question – what can I allow myself? Can I allow myself space in the wardrobe, in the bed, in my own life? Would expansion into his wardrobe mean I was accepting his non-return? Accepting that this is solely my house now and I don't have to make space for him? Does it mean I'm 'moving on', which still feels unbearable? Does it mean I'm somehow 'profiting' from his death?

I can't bear to think that my life could be better in any way without him. Irrational as it seems, having a tidier, more spacious wardrobe, which would in many ways be better, feels in this moment almost as bad as having an affair: an emotional betrayal, a giving up on him. I can't have a better life without him.

Of course, rationally I know no one, least of all him, would ever think I could seriously take the small relief of neatly arranged shoes as adequate compensation for lifelong companionship and love with my soulmate, but in the disordered state of grieving, these things take on massive significance. If it's this hard to put my shoes where his once were, how likely is it that I would ever let another person in? These tiny steps destroy me and fling me backwards. I don't want to move on, I don't want to have my life eased in any way. He has no life, so how dare I have even a slightly easier one? And it has thrown up another decision – when and how do I get rid of his clothes? Of all the massive decisions I need to make, that one feels huge. The one and only time I have opened his wardrobe since his death was to choose a suit for him to wear in his coffin, and that nearly undid me. I had to abort mission and leave it to my mother to sort in my place. There is something so poignant about empty suits that he will never wear, some still revealing echoes of his presence – in the signs of bagginess around the place his knees once bent and crossed, the worn patches where his elbows once resided, the faint stains of spilled food, or the remnants of his smell.

The wardrobe dilemma feels so symbolic of the compromises you make as a couple and how decisions aren't meant to be made unilaterally in intertwined lives. There's a weird feeling that I can't move into his space because that would make it hard to go back to sharing – as though he will be coming back. There's a resistance to accepting the finality of it and what taking up some of his space would represent: that he's really gone, that I am alone in this bedroom. And a realisation that

I will never live with anyone else, a sense of unwelcome responsibility that this house, this life is entirely mine to do what I want with. I don't need to take anyone else into account and can be completely selfish. But how unnatural and unhealthy that feels. And frightening. Like a child left home alone too early, who craves boundaries and restrictions in order to feel safe and contained. To keep that chaos at bay.

Yet as the days pass and I let the wardrobe situation percolate, I notice that there are signs of movement. I was going to say progress, but that's not right – it's not progress, which suggests 'better', it's just 'change', which has no negative or positive connotations. At first I could move nothing. I kept everything exactly where it always had been. I didn't necessarily look at them, but they were there in my peripheral vision – shaving brush, razor, toothbrush, old notes on bedside table, half-read book, his glasses, his watch.

But this morning I threw away the shaving brush and soap. I rationalised that the brush was worn out and needed replacing and the soap was on its last legs too. Whether they really were or not was irrelevant – but somehow, thinking that they were due to be thrown out soon anyway, that felt okay to my warped and irrational logic. So, without consciously making a decision, I just grabbed them and threw them in the bin and kept walking. Didn't mull, didn't cry, just did it as though it was the most normal thing in the world. Just tidying up a few things nearing the end of their shelf life. No big deal. Nothing to see here.

So now there is a tiny bit more space on the basin. Two items that were there, gone. Removing them by stealth, pretending I'm not noticing myself doing it. Creating space. Funny how often that word crops up. Literal space, both welcome and unwelcome. Space in my life, in my heart – no, not that; if anything there is less space in my heart because he's grown in stature in there. But space for me. If I want it, which I don't. Space also to grieve in a more open way, more expansively maybe. I'm no longer in the locked-down frozen, shocked, numb, closed state of those early days. I've been trying to reclaim my body, have attempted the occasional yoga class. I've even allowed myself to look at photos and started to let myself think beyond the next minute occasionally. When I cry it's heart-rending and feels unstoppable, but it's coming out more and more often. And of course, it is better out than in.

With cracks appearing in my composure it feels like time to address this crumbling of the carapace. With feelings breaking through the shield of denial more and more often, I am struggling to cope. I need to let myself be with what is coming up for me, but I need to do that in a safe and holding environment where I won't feel so alone with it.

In a rather odd and synchronous twist of fate I am asked to review a retreat all about loss, taking place in the depths of the Somerset countryside. Before I was a psychotherapist, when I wrote and directed television programmes, I also had occasional work as a travel writer for newspapers, and also for the website Queen of Retreats. Although I'd stopped most of my journalistic endeavours when I became a therapist, I had clung on to the reviewing part, taking one or two trips a year to experience new retreats – yoga, fitness, relaxation, detox or meditation – and I really enjoyed keeping that writer part of me alive.

Knowing of my situation, the Queen of Retreats' founder has suggested I go on a grief retreat called 'The Bridge'. I'll be there to review it, of course, but also because it might help me with my loss. I am sceptical and reluctant, to say the least. This is not to be a fluffy-towel, soothing-massages and gentle-downward-dog sort of a retreat. This is to be a full-on, immersive, twelve-hour-a-day-confrontation-with-your-demons sort of a retreat. I hate the idea. But part of me – grown-up therapist me – also knows that my strong resistance is probably a sign of how necessary it is for me to do this. I have spent the preceding months veering wildly from moments of complete meltdown to moments of frantic distracting activity, and back again; I know how badly I need to rebalance myself by shutting out the outside world and properly spending quality time with my feelings and memories. But I also know how painful that is going to be – there is a reason that I've been trying to avoid just such a scenario. One of the things I am most nervous about is the handing over of my phone and iPad on the way in. Reading, listening to podcasts and texting have been the only things getting me through the long, unbearable nights of insomnia. But hand them in I do. Physical props removed, distractions forbidden, friends uncontactable, I face down my fellow retreaters and prepare to also face down my pain and fear.

The group gathers and the ten of us tell our stories of loss, one by one. We've each been asked to kick off our tales by introducing an object that represents what it is we have lost.

Floating

I have brought a ring that I used to wear on my wedding ring finger, which broke just a few months before Bill died. My official wedding and engagement rings are small and cheap, at my insistence. Back when we'd first been planning our wedding I hadn't wanted extravagant rings – I thought they were unnecessary, and I had never been a jewellery wearer and wasn't even sure if I wanted to be 'branded' in the way that a wedding ring symbolises. But I thought I'd give wearing one a go, see if I could be converted, and chose the cheapest, thinnest one I could find in case I hated it.

Eventually I gave in to convention after repeatedly being asked to 'show off' my engagement ring and seeing the look of disappointment on people's faces when they couldn't enthuse over such a poor specimen. Bill said he wanted to buy me a nicer one, if and when I found one I liked. This we eventually did in a vintage fair in Southwold a few months after we were married – which is why I don't really know how to name this ring that I wore on my wedding finger, but which only arrived after the event. It's a 1920s French platinum ring in the shape of a flower with diamonds as petals. It is beautiful, but it was made for a softer type of woman in a softer type of age, and its vintage meant it was unsuited to my life of gardening, cooking, washing up and public transport. The band eventually wore through. A jeweller assessed it as being un-repairable, so Bill said that the next time we were feeling flush he would get me another one. Obviously that didn't happen, and I can hardly buy myself one now – that would be too weird – so I can't help but see this broken ring as yet another metaphor for my life at the moment – old one broken, yet a new one unimaginable and just somehow wrong.

I use this broken symbol to introduce myself to the group. Will this retreat do a better job of patching me up than the jeweller who gave up so easily on the ring?

Turns out, it does.

Confronting the demons is bloody awful, but it does help. Over the course of the six-day retreat, in the company of this equally terrified group of fellow travellers, I sob, shout and scream my way through the mass of feelings that have been churning away both internally and, intermittently, externally for months. That I feel safe to do so is thanks so the two amazing therapists who lead and hold the group so steadfastly.

~

As a psychotherapist, I'm clearly not exactly a neutral voice here. And, as a psychotherapist, I have completely signed up to the number one ground rule of psychotherapy – we do not give advice. But I'm not actually in a psychotherapeutic relationship with any of you, so I'm going to ignore all that for one moment, break the rules of the game, go out on a limb and advise that seeing a therapist can be a really useful thing to do after a bereavement. And the closer the relationship with the person who died, and the more traumatic the death, the more useful a therapist is likely to be.

I have had a lot of therapy in my life, both in my twenties and thirties when I was often quite unhappy, and confused by why I was so, and throughout my six years of training to become a therapist myself, when it was a requirement of the course.

And I can honestly say that therapy has transformed my life in more ways than I can possibly articulate.

Having a therapist is not the same as having good friends and family you can speak to. Having a therapist is not the same as having read a good self-help book, or books about the history of psychotherapy, or academic books about psychotherapy. Having a therapist is not the same as going on antidepressants. It is not the same as finding solace in music, or art, or a walk in nature, or religion, or meditation, or yoga or exercise. It is not the same as anything else at all, fantastic though all those other things are. And yet many, many people tell me that they don't need therapy because they have one or all of the above, or because they have just never felt the need for it.

I happen to believe that we all need therapy at some points in our lives, not just when bereaved. But especially when bereaved.

Even with all the years of therapy I have had over the course of my life, even with all my hard-earned therapeutic knowledge and academic training, even having a vast army of friends who are therapists, I still went for some bereavement counselling after Bill's death. It was only for ten weeks, yet that weekly session, over those two and a half months, gave me space and time with a completely uninvolved, independent, skilled, trained person by my side, to work with my feelings in a way that all the friends, books, or music in the world cannot offer. It was incredibly useful and necessary.

Losing someone is hard, losing someone is traumatic, losing someone is not a single moment in time after which you can cry a bit, brush yourself off, pop a pill or two and go back to how you were. It is a full body, mind, brain and emotionally turbulent explosion that rocks your entire world and all your beliefs, and after which you will never be the same again. That's not to suggest that the new you can't be wonderful and find lots of joy and happiness, but it is not the same you. I believe we can all benefit from professional help to accompany us through such a change, to help us get to know this new person – or more accurately, people, if you subscribe to the multiple selves theory, as I do – who are residing in our bodies.

With the therapists at the retreat, I do indeed find myself able to access some of the harder-to-reach, deeper emotions I'd been frightened of accessing alone. They have created a space safe enough that I can allow myself to acknowledge how deeply Bill's loss has affected me, and also to recognise the many corollary losses brought in its wake. If I were to list them, and in no particular order, those losses might go something like this: I have lost love; my closest companion and confidant; my reason for living; my future; my sense of self; my sense of identity; my sense of purpose; my optimism; my feeling of safety; my figure. Okay, so maybe that last one makes it seem like the list is descending into triviality, but do you know what? These things do matter. In the overall scheme of things, of course losing my figure is nowhere near the biggest loss I've had to face, and it's understandable that I've been eating my way through the pain, but I'm trying to be honest here – losing my figure hurts! Losing the 'shape' that I identify as me does feel like another bereavement of sorts. I don't recognise myself when I look in the mirror, I don't like what I now see there and, when combined with the disappearance of all the other things that similarly went into giving me a solid sense of self, it doesn't feel trivial to me to be thrown by this. Bill, of course, wouldn't have cared less what size I grew to, ever, and it feels so ironic that just when I am approaching fifty, and menopausal, and losing my figure and my looks, I no longer have the person who would nevertheless have always found me beautiful, whatever the visual evidence to the contrary.

It makes me realise more than ever what a big loss uncon-ditional love is. I know Bill would have barely even noticed my ageing. And he would have, and did, put up with all my grumpiness and my bad moods, and my boring repetitive stories. As I put up with his, because in a good relationship you love each other for your flaws as much as you love each other for the good bits. No one else signed that contract allow-ing me to be me in all my worst moments as well as my best ones, throughout the good, bad and ugly; a contract to continue to love me throughout. And of course, I mean the emotional contract, not literally the marriage contract. I have lost the person who put me first. Just as Bill was my world, so was I his, so I have lost feeling like the most special, the most important person in someone's life. No one else will ever be so intimately involved or care about me as much as Bill did. I'm not the centre of anyone's world. No one's life will be irrevoca-bly changed without me in it. I am less important. I matter less. I realise how alone I am as never before. All sorts of ques-tions start arising: whose name do I put as my emergency contact on my passport? Who do I call if I have a stroke? Who will organise my funeral? Who will administer my will and sort through my possessions? Who will make decisions for me if I get Alzheimer's?

I also feel I have lost my connection to my own body. From the moment Bill first clutched his chest my own body has been clenched tight, held in against the pain. Rationally, my therapist self has been aware of this and of the need to address it, but my grieving self, fighting to stay afloat, hasn't felt anywhere near ready to take on board a physical inventory alongside everything else she's been grappling with. When I've felt able to, I've dragged myself to a few yoga classes, done a tiny bit of walking, a tiny bit of cycling, but the most exercise I've had has been lifting my hand to my mouth to shovel in more food. But here at The Bridge I do gradually start to physically unfreeze, and with this comes the thawing of yet more, yet deeper emotions. The two are so connected. During my decades of practising yoga I have seen this many times – as the body starts to release, so too does the stored-up emotion. I've been in yoga classes in which people, myself included, have been happily transitioning through various poses, only to suddenly find that a particular shape has unleashed a torrent of unsuspected tears. This deep connection between body and mind is foregrounded in yet another branch of psychotherapy – body psychotherapy.

~

Fundamental to the body psychotherapy approach is the understanding that body and mind are indivisible and that each influences the other bidirectionally. Reading the body, working with the body, sensing into the body – all of these are important elements to include.

Most of us readily accept that our emotions can have a physical manifestation – embarrassment causes our cheeks to go red, nervousness causes butterflies to fly around in our stomachs, fear causes our hands or knees to shake and joy causes a burst of noise known as laughter to issue from our bellies via our vocal cords.

And yet we seem to find it hard to look beyond these most obvious physical signs and understand that all our experiences, our ways of being and relating, our personalities, can also be written in our bodies, and that our bodies are in turn shaping our ways of being in the world. We do know it on some level – much of our language reveals exactly how embodied we are: we say that we need to 'stand on our own two feet', 'get some backbone', 'swallow it down', or that we've 'had a bellyful' of someone and need to 'stand up for ourselves'. There are myriad ways in which we acknowledge how symbolic our bodies are, how much they mirror personality traits we wish we did or didn't have more of.

Bodies can't lie the way our minds can. Body language can tell us so much about what a person is really thinking – the unconsciously jerking foot possibly indicating a suppressed anger behind a person's calm soothing speech, the arms defensively folded across the chest of someone made vulnerable by having been asked a personal question, the tapping fingers of someone impatient to move on to the next subject. Therapists know how to tune in to these unspoken messages.

Remember Bowlby's notion of internal working models – those rules we have absorbed so fully into our belief systems and our behaviours that we come to believe they are just 'how I am'? Body psychotherapists believe that these models are not just printed on our minds, behaviours and emotions, but are also embodied; that is to say, rendered manifest in our bodies. Some, most even, are subtle, but some can be read there quite visibly – think of someone whose internal message to themselves has always been that they are worthless and not worth listening to. That person will more than likely have adopted a body posture that folds in on itself, as though trying to take up as little space as possible in the world, to make themselves so small as to be almost invisible. Or someone who has always been afraid but tries to hide their fear behind a defensive chest-out, chin-forward sort of a stance to make themselves look bigger. This is a classic defence made physical – this person's body may well be saying 'You will not get close enough to me to hurt me because I will hurt you first.' A depressed person is another good example: you can often see in their posture that they are literally weighed down by their despair, hunched as though the world is on their shoulders, head bowed because they can't face the world.

Like so many branches of psychotherapy, this way of thinking about how we operate began with Freud, whose initial theory very much included the body before he jettisoned it in favour of the supremacy of the mind. It was later returned to and taken up by others who further developed the idea. Wilhelm Reich, and later Alexander Lowen, talked in terms of body armouring. They believed strongly that the defences discovered by Freud translated into actual physical ways of holding the body and lodged in the muscles – we are literally armouring ourselves against our fears. They saw the aim of therapy as being to physically release those muscles using various exercises, and that by doing so long-held emotions would be unleashed along with them, just as I had seen many times in yoga, and had experienced in dancing at the ceilidh.

This physical release of tension is rarely used in the therapy room nowadays and constitutes only one aspect of body psychotherapy. There are many other, more common, tools in the body psychotherapist's arsenal, many of which relate to communication both intra- and inter-personally. On the intrapersonal level, if we have lost, or never quite found, how to relate to ourselves, then relating to others becomes harder. Body psychotherapists will encourage you to sense into your body, connect with it, become mindful of its messages and use them to achieve better mind/body communication and understanding.

Learning to connect with your body in this way can be very painful if you have gone through a massive trauma; and some grief, especially sudden grief, can be categorised as trauma. Decades of research have revealed just how long-lasting are the effects of trauma on the body. Books by pioneering thera-pists Bessel Van der Kolk, *The Body Keeps the Score*, and Babette Rothschild, *The Body Remembers*, both testify to the embodied nature of trauma, while their research and clinical experience prove how it can detrimentally affect so much – the immune system, the muscular, skeletal, endocrine and respiratory systems, the ability to tolerate connection, the propensity to dissociate, all of which can lead to extreme hyper- and hypo-arousal responses. Given such profound effects it is understandable that connecting to the body might be the last thing you feel like doing. Why open that Pandora's box of pain by attempting mindful connection? The tempta-tion to shut yourself off from your physical sensations, as with other forms of denial, is understandable and can, for a while, be a life-saving way of not allowing yourself to be swept away by the overwhelm. But get too used to it and you might forget to let yourself feel again, forget to breathe again even.

I noticed after my father's death, and then in a much greater way after Bill's, that a lot of my unexpressed emotion embedded itself physically. My body felt very heavy; I was lugging it around, there was no energy, no vitality. Once again I am struck by the literalness of this expression – I could feel no vitality – a word that comes from 'vita', meaning life. Without it my body was manifestly revealing how little I really wanted life, how much of me had died along with Bill and how little the rest of me wanted to remain here without him.

What energy I could muster was going into just surviving – holding it together emotionally, practically – and very physically, in that I was gripping my muscles, clenching everything I had. I didn't know I was doing this, but I did know that I was tired all the time. Beyond tired, exhausted to my very bones. This was also partly due to the insomnia that was a constant unwelcome addition to my life, but the completely shattered weariness that dogged me felt more metaphorical, definitely a tired-of-life sort of a tiredness. Exercise, usually so fundamental to my existence, couldn't have been further from what it used to be, a joy. Instead it felt like an impossibility. This was yet another way in which I didn't recognise myself – the person who used to look forward to a run, or a yoga class, or a bike ride; that person felt a complete stranger to me now. What a chore all those things seemed. And the less I did them, the less I wanted to do them and the more divorced from my body I got. Mindfulness or any sort of connecting with this strange form now masquerading as my body felt completely impossible. Why would I want to do that?

But the movement exercises at the retreat helped dislodge some of that, helped me realise that I did still have a body, however unrecognisable it felt. And at the same time the mindfulness sessions – the act of, conversely, staying still with my body and listening to what it was trying to tell me – also helped me reconnect and understand how alienated my body was from my mind.

Just as the body is a source of information as to what you have been through, so it can be a source of change. The more I let the therapists open my mind and heart to the pain, the more my body could unclench and open. And the more my body opened, the more my mind and emotions could release a bit further themselves. A happy feedback loop. Well, maybe happy is pushing it, but a feedback loop nonetheless.

If an existentialist approach helped carve a path towards making meaning, then a body psychotherapy approach helps open new channels of connection – towards myself and towards others. I think that one of the things that has always appealed to me about body psychotherapy is that so much of it chimes with what I already know from twenty-five years of practising yoga. The parallels are there: in the acceptance of the body and mind as a unified, interconnected whole equally deserving of attention; in the commitment to mindfulness and sensing inwards; and in the acknowledgement of the need for proper grounding. Attachment theory explained to us the psychological need to have a 'secure base' from which to explore. Both body psychotherapy and yoga render this theory literal, with their emphasis on securely rooting and grounding – via your feet and the sensations within – to the securest base of all, the Earth.

Without healthy roots anchored in the Earth we cannot grow. The deeper a tree's roots, the higher will its branches extend. And the same is true for us. In yoga you always start with your connection to the floor. The more you can ground and find your roots, the higher will your backbends fly, your headstands, your balances. Whenever you want to reach in yoga, you root first – and that grounding enables growth. In therapy the same is true – anchor yourself in a safe relationship with a therapist who can become your secure base and the exploration comes naturally.

And so it is for me here at the Bridge retreat in Somerset. I am learning to re-find some stability, physically and emotionally. Even my ongoing inner visualisation of being in the ocean has shifted accordingly. I am still far from land, but the turbulence has calmed, the sun is peeking through the clouds onto a flatter, less violent sea and the ragged pieces of wood I've been clinging to till now have floated me towards a boat. A small one, let's say a canoe-sized one, but a boat nevertheless. The Bridge gives me the energy to clamber aboard. I no longer have to grip and hold myself quite so tightly but instead, for the first time in a long time, can feel what it's like to have something solid beneath my feet, even if the boat itself doesn't yet have anything solid beneath it.

In this long horrible grief journey, I'll take any little improvements I can get. It's a rather wobbly solidity here on ever-shifting waters, and I'm still very much at the mercy of the elements, but it provides a measure of stability that I have not had till now. As I yield into the support beneath me, and root more deeply into my bodily sensations, just as in yoga, that anchoring allows me to reach a bit more expansively, both physically and metaphorically. With deeper roots burrowing downwards, I find that my branches can reach higher – to the sky, to the transcendent. The connection to my body helps me discern a connection to something more 'out of body', something more spiritual.

~

On the first day of the holistic activity holiday in Skyros where Bill and I met, we were taken on a tour of the property. Rather randomly – or maybe not so randomly in rural Greece – we came across a sunbathing pig. Bill and I both found ourselves stopping to stroke this friendly, relaxed creature, who took evident delight in the attention.

Two years later in his characteristically funny wedding speech Bill joked about us having stroked a pig together on the first day we met.

Fast-forward to now and me here alone at the Bridge retreat, 'dealing' with Bill's death. In the paddock opposite the farmhouse where I sleep are two pigs, one male, one female – a couple, we are told. I love them. They seem like a little humorous message put there by Billy to make me laugh and remind me of our first meeting, and of his wedding speech. I go out and talk to them regularly. The male lets me stroke him, the female is shyer.

I've already talked about the various happenings at and around his funeral that I found strange, and how, whether or not you believe these to be real signs, to me they absolutely do feel like messages from Bill.

I have a couple more too.

When Bill was about eighteen, he taught geography for a few terms at a small private school in a Shropshire village, Kinlet. He stayed in touch with the family who owned and ran the school, even to the point of continuing to receive and read the monthly village newsletter for the rest of his life. I was feeling sad one day that I hadn't had a 'message' from Bill in a while, so in my nightly chat to him I asked him to send another. Two days later I opened my post to find a cheque for twenty pounds. Turns out Bill had not only been continuing to subscribe to the Kinlet newsletter, he had also been making regular donations to its raffle. He had won that month's draw.

After Bill's mother died, he and his siblings had to clear her house, a mammoth task that was still ongoing after his own death. I returned to the house on a couple of occasions to help my sisters-in-law continue the seemingly never-ending clear-out. One day I came across a little metal tin, from the fifties perhaps, that had once contained something called 'Sure Shield Iodised Throat Lozenges'. I asked my sister-in-law if I could keep it and she of course said yes and told me she'd just found a similar tin containing 'Gee's Linctus Pastilles'. I took them both home and put them on the mantelpiece. A few weeks later, going through Bill's phone photos, I came across a photo of that very same Gee's linctus pastilles tin. All I could think was that he had photographed it with the intention of going back for it later, or possibly to show me to ask if it was something I might like (he knew me so well). He never had the chance to bring the tin home, and yet here it is, on our mantelpiece.

These signs, 'real' or not, are so, so comforting to me. And they seem so necessary for helping me believe Bill is okay, doing well, still laughing, still with me, still joking, still looking out for me.

Back to the pigs. Imagine my horror when on day four of the retreat I look out of the window and see them being loaded onto a trailer. I am utterly devastated. I cannot bear to think these pigs that were sent to me by Bill to make me laugh, and which have given me such pleasure, are about to be sent to slaughter. How could the universe be so cruel? I sob and sob, completely undone.

And then one of the staff tells me the porcine pair have merely been moved to a nearby field. Their job is to move around from field to field churning up the ground, rejuvenating old stuck mud and creating movement and space with their burrowing trotters, to create a fertile environment and rich foundation for new growth. And the meadow that I had previously been watching them in is now destined to be a wildflower meadow – my favourite sight in the world and the seeds of which would now fall on more fertile ground, thanks to those pigs.

Oh, my joy in the symbolism of it all! My fear of their demise, followed by the comforting revelation that they are staying together, heading off to new pastures . . .

Now of course 'gone to another field' does sound suspiciously like the 'gone to live on a farm' story told to children when their parents can't bring themselves to tell them that a beloved pet has died. While I'm not sure a 'grief retreat' predicated on helping us confront our losses face-on could really peddle that line and retain any credibility whatsoever, I can't know for certain.

And therein lies the rub. I cannot know for definite whether those pigs have really gone to truffle happily around the next field creating wildflower meadows of the future, or whether they are in fact now upside down on a butcher's hook. But really, does it matter what the literal truth is? I can either sob with pain thinking about the brutal reality of most pigs' life cycle, or I can feel uplifted, warm and hopeful imagining them snuffling around their new field together, wild flowers trailing in their wake. And if I choose to see that as some sort of allegory for Bill and me, a message he has sent me, then who am I hurting by opting for this interpretation?

I choose to focus on the fact that one of the most interesting changes for me, since Bill's death, is my openness to the idea of another realm beyond this one and, more broadly, a more spiritual life view.

And that often happens after a death. Those left behind, scrabbling as they are to make sense of their loss and rediscover an identity without their loved one, often find that their views on spirituality and the afterlife change. Some people who had been very religious lose their faith in the face of the betrayal they feel at losing their loved one unfairly; others with no previous faith find it. Devout Christian C. S. Lewis's memoir of losing his wife, Joy – *A Grief Observed*, later made into the film and play *Shadowlands* – sees him wrestling with his religious beliefs hand in hand with his grief. For him the two cannot be separated.

For my part, my previously rather woolly and unformed notions of a world beyond start to clarify and I find myself becoming increasingly convinced that there is so much more than just this material world. And, funnily enough, there is a branch of therapy that addresses just this.

~

Like many of the therapeutic approaches I have written about here, transpersonal therapy can offer another way of thinking about and being with grief, another language with which to try to understand loss.

Spirituality is a massively important subject to many people, obviously for those who have it or are open to it, but equally for those who are virulently against it or just uninterested. Any of those are valid and acceptable choices. This is true for life in general but is never truer than when grieving. Please, please feel free to believe in whatever works for you, whether that be a belief that death is the cold hard end with nothing afterwards and with no higher power either above or below; a belief in an all-powerful God in white robes; or anything in between. Not knowing is also fine. As Shakespeare's Hamlet says, 'There are more things in heaven and earth, Horatio, than are dreamt of in your philosophy'.

Like Hamlet, transpersonal therapy allows for the notion that there may be things 'out there' of which we cannot dream – nor perhaps imagine or rationally explain. Loosely, it seeks to encompass the notion that we are all interconnected and part of a bigger whole. The prefix 'trans' in this context comes from the word 'beyond' – beyond the personal, beyond this material world, beyond the individual ego, beyond space and time.

Famous names who have worked within this framework are Carl Jung, Stanislav Grof, Ken Wilber, Roberto Assagioli, Abraham Maslow and John Rowan.

Transpersonal therapy doesn't necessarily need to be religious or philosophical, although it might be if the client has their own faith that they wish to bring into it, but it is characterised by the fact that it acknowledges that something transcendent exists, whichever words one might use to describe that – the spirit, the soul, the universe, the truth, the light, the sacred, numinous, holy, or divine.

The options are many but show how difficult it is to articulate, categorise or pin down something so nebulous, something that is more felt than thought. In this way I feel it to be similar to grief itself, which also tends to reside within, have shape and form within one's very cells and hormones, and is difficult to grasp intellectually, let alone put into words.

Believing in something beyond this world – in whatever way is meaningful to you – can provide another path through the anarchy into which grief has plunged you. It can help you find a higher purpose behind your suffering, enable you to take some comfort from the thought that even if you don't know what the hell is going on, some higher power does, that he/she/it has a master plan that makes sense of what just happened and will go on to happen. Religion, or a broader spiritual faith, provides this for some people. Transpersonal therapy can help you explore whether faith in any kind of 'beyond' might help you find some clarity, if clarity is lacking.

This therapy acknowledges the need to be present with our suffering. It asks that we confront all our deepest darkest fears, learn to be with them and allow for the fact that there are things that we cannot always control. This knowledge is impossible to avoid when you have lost a loved one, making a transpersonal approach very relevant to the bereaved.

Confronting our pain in this way is fundamental to most therapeutic approaches, but each approach has its own take, and its own way of emphasising what is most important. Others may focus more on our day-to-day experience, or on relationship, or on our inner worlds, as opposed to viewing us through the wider transpersonal lens.

Just as many philosophical elements of transpersonal therapy cross over into other methods, so too do some of the ways one might go about working with whatever arises. For instance, techniques such as meditation, working with dreams, visualisations, mythology and storytelling are used by many therapeutic approaches, but they feature particularly strongly in the transpersonal field. Again, I feel these are things that seem to naturally come to the fore – in some of us at least – when grieving, possibly due to the inadequacies of word-based language in conveying such complexity of response. The language of myth and metaphor can often be more eloquent. My own deeply felt sense of being adrift in the ocean, and my ability to somehow find a metaphor for my tumultuous feelings therein, speaks to this need for visualisation and imagery.

So much has changed since Bill died. My inner world, my outer world and my relationship with a realm 'beyond' are all shifting and being reassessed. It may be that a more transpersonal approach could be something I will take more on board from now on in my professional life, when I eventually return to it. It's certainly already causing changes in my personal life.

Since Bill died I have felt his presence so strongly that I have to recognise that I now believe in 'another realm' more than ever. Deep down I always have, I think, but up until his death, my spiritual journey was rather cursory, meandering and flaky. Mum was a disinterested Presbyterian, Dad a lapsed Catholic, I was mainly secular state-school educated ... I knew next to nothing about any religion at all growing up, apart from the occasional visit to church at Christmas and Easter. That suited me fine as I am not good with authority, nor with tradition or ritual, and I hate dogma of any kind. I associate all these things with religion, so it had never really entered my world. But I had always had a bit of an inkling that there had to be something more than just this realm, even if I could never have articulated what this sensation was.

Bill and I had dabbled in Buddhism as this seemed to us to come closest to what we sort-of-believed but never really fully engaged with. We loved the philosophy, the absence of dogma and the sense of personal responsibility alongside public compassion. It was definitely feeding something in us, but it was also lacking in something we couldn't put our finger on.

I needed more engagement. This seemed to be not only around a need for more spiritual guidance, or a framework at least, but also around needing to feel I belonged somewhere. When I left the television industry I left behind a 'tribe', a community to which I'd belonged since university, a place that had itself been a community, as had school before that. I'd always felt I belonged somewhere, was part of a team, had a structure supporting me. I'd gone on to find a similar sense of community and belonging among my fellow students while training as a psychotherapist. But when I graduated and started working in private practice on my own in my house, I suddenly felt adrift and alone. My father was very ill at this time and, not being close to my mother or sister, it felt a very isolating time. I no longer had workmates, and soon would have – with my father's inevitable death ahead – precious little family. I started worrying that if anything happened to Bill (ha! If I'd known!) I would be one of those people you hear about on the news whose body is only discovered two years after their death because no one had noticed they were missing and they'd been half eaten by their cats.

It was when I was in the midst of this rather precarious state of mind that Bill and I found ourselves at our local Quaker Meeting House.

Our favourite weekend every year was always London's Open House Weekend, when the city throws open its doors to those interested in architecture, enabling a backstage peek behind the facades of some of London's most architecturally fascinating buildings. And this particular year, the year when I was feeling most isolated in my career, most disillusioned with Buddhism and very afraid at the inevitable loss of my dad, we visited the Quaker Meeting House in Hammersmith. We looked round the building and got chatting to one of the elders, who told us not only the architectural story, but a bit about Quakerism itself. It sounded right up our street. We learned that Quakers are basically rebels at heart, although I'm not sure how much some would thank me for that interpretation. Some would, however, because above all else they

allow for – were even founded upon – the notions of dissent and discussion. Most importantly for us, they are non-dogmatic. They don't require you necessarily to believe in God, or the Bible and they are liberal, non-hierarchical, environmentalist, pacifist, non-judgemental, activist – all the things that we also believed ourselves to be. We learned that they met every Sunday for an hour of, mostly, silent worship, although if anyone feels moved by what they discover within themselves during that silent communion with their inner faith, then they are free to 'minister' and share it with the group.

They also clearly have a strong sense of community and a care for others, the very thing I'd been craving, and which had felt lacking from the Buddhist group we'd been going to. The clue's in the title – their official name is the 'Religious Society of Friends', for goodness sake!

'Let's start going to Meetings,' said Bill as we left.

'Okay,' I said. And we did.

A few weeks after that, a card landed on our doorstep. At first I couldn't make head nor tail of it – it was signed with a whole load of names I didn't recognise and it told me not to worry, I wasn't alone, I was now part of the Quaker community. I soon worked out that this was one of Bill's mad inventions to cheer me up. He had made the card and posted it to me, having fabricated the names of imagined Quakers – we hadn't yet got to know the real people – and was pretending this was a card from the future that I might one day receive, giving me reassurance that were I to be left alone, this new group of people we didn't really know yet might be there for me.

'They'll make sure the cats don't eat you if you die without me there,' he said when I asked him what on earth the card meant.

Bill's empathy in understanding what I was going through, his unusual and creative ways of trying to reassure me, his compassion and his absurd humour, were what made him so extraordinary. And this card was, I think, also the first of many signs, a prescience about what might happen to us. And sure enough, after he died I did indeed get just such a card, this time filled with the real names of real people whom I had come to know and love, and who are indeed there for me.

I think there is another imperative behind my deepening belief in a world beyond, which I have to articulate like this: I cannot bear to think that Bill has just disappeared, that nothing of him remains. He was too wonderful, and unique and amazing, for all that to have just evaporated into thin air. He cannot have worked so hard and done such good in his life, and yet been cheated of any sort of earthly reward, without there being rewards of another, hopefully greater kind, in store for him instead. I have to believe he is happy and at peace. More than at peace – in bliss. I don't know what bliss means but I want him to have it. I need him to have it. I need to believe that his 'life' now is one of freedom from pain and worry, full of beer and cake, cricket and foot-ball, and people who laugh at his jokes. If I don't have that thought to hang on to then I really cannot keep going. He can't have lived in vain. He just can't. I won't allow it. And I don't think he will allow me to follow that negative train of thought either. I think that is what lies behind the silly, funny, cheeky messages that he continues to send me. As he has done recently – from inside a Quaker Meeting.

Five years on from that first visit to Hammersmith Meeting House, the weekly Meeting for Worship has become an important part of my life. One morning, as I sat meditating there, I felt sadness arise very strongly, and I asked Billy to send me a sign that he was okay and happy. As I opened my eyes I was struck by the image on the front cover of a book being read by a Friend sitting directly opposite. The word was FOREST, in large letters, standing out against a background picture of a forest. Now, Bill was a lifelong Nottingham Forest supporter, so that word, and related items (a Forest mug, a Forest scarf, a Forest jigsaw, Forest memorabilia . . .), loomed large in our house: 'Forest's won, Forest's lost, Forest's playing next week, Forest's on telly, Forest's not on telly . . .' Bill also loved actual forests and had raised a lot of money for the Woodland Trust.

All of which is to say this felt like another request answered. The really weird thing is that generally people don't read in Meeting, apart from maybe *Quaker Faith and Practice*, our spiritual textbook, or the Bible, or spiritual texts from other religions, but I have never before or since seen anyone read anything other than these few texts during Meeting.

Events like this are what lead me to say that I now believe ever more firmly that there has to be more to this world than just this world. Of course, it could be simply because I can't bear to think that someone so extraordinary and so essential to me has just evaporated into nothingness; that I delude myself with the comforting thought that he still exists somewhere, and I therefore look for scenarios that confirm this bias. I don't think that's the reason; I like to believe that they are more than that. And if that makes me feel happier when I'm down, and keeps me feeling connected to Billy – well, it might be madness, but it's a madness that keeps me sane.

Chapter Five

Balancing

Alongside my deepening connection to the spiritual world comes its counterweight – a re-engagement with the couldn't-be-more-material world; with its earthly pleasures; with hedonism even. I wonder if this suggests that there is a part of me now wanting to live a bit more expansively. To live life, in fact, as opposed to the sort of half-life I've been flailing about in.

With the gradual loosening up of my body and mind, and the intense offloading of heavy emotions that the Bridge retreat unleashed, I am starting to feel a bit freer. The remote controller also seems to be loosening his grip. He is no longer such a sadist and I am slowly regaining a modicum of self-control, over my emotions at least, if not over my behaviour: in that arena I have noticed a new version of me coming into being, a hitherto unknown self who behaves rather erratically and in occasionally rather worrying ways. She is taking centre stage more often and I need to get to know her better. I fear a more sensible me may need to step in soon, but for now I think all my more predictable selves are rather enjoying her odd, sometimes carefree and occasionally somewhat reckless behaviour. For now, at least, my better-known selves are giving her free rein and urging 'you go girl'.

*   *   *

This new self's mantra seems to run something like this: life has dealt me a really shitty fucking hand, and I for one am not having it. What happened to me sucks, so whatever I want to do, I'm bloody well allowed to do it: eat more chocolate, drink more cocktails, go on more holidays, please my damn self in whatever way I choose. I deserve some compensation for my shitty luck. If I'm not allowed children, or a husband, or a family, then I'm going to bloody well enjoy whatever I can and consume whatever I feel I am allowed. Which right now is anything I damn well want. Nothing is off limits. And no one – certainly not my Scottish Presbyterian bank manager self – is going to stop me.

In fact, I'm locking that one in her dressing room and not allowing her out for quite a long time. With her out of the way I notice two unfamiliar behaviours becoming quite dominant.

Firstly, I find that I am excessively tidying and arranging and moving things. That's not the reckless bit – I'm not so sad that I think housework constitutes a rock and roll lifestyle – but it is a different type of behaviour from normal so I'll start there.

Part of this new behaviour is practical and necessary. The chaos that has been building up since Bill's death has left me unable to face simple things like housework, and, as I have started to finally remove some of his possessions and move my own around, the house has been pretty chaotic and messy – a visible reflection of my disordered mind. So there does actually need to be some rearranging and tidying. But I seem to be a woman possessed, endlessly moving things from room to room, 'getting organised', packing and unpacking bags and

boxes of stuff, as though by rearranging the house I am subli-
mating (another Freudian defence) my unmet need to rearrange my identity. It's really just the latest version of my
attempts to create order and control out of a disordered
universe. Of course, we all know that tendency – normally
when a piece of work is due – to discover an urgent need to
neaten your underwear drawer or clean the cutlery tray, but I
realise it is getting slightly pathological when I find myself
tidying the tea bag caddy. I'm trying to line up the teabags like
soldiers into their different brands, which had all got mixed
up together. As if it matters. They are all just variations on
bog-standard builder's tea, but it seems important not only to
separate them out into their relevant tribes, but also to make
them stand up on their edges. This is teabags I am corralling.
Possibly not quite within the realms of normal behaviour.

The second, conceivably related, new behaviour is
unchecked retail therapy. I've never been a big shopper. Hate
it in fact. Hate the experience of it, the materialism, the trudg-
ing, the bags, the decisions, but also hate spending unnecessary money. I have quite a puritanical approach, possibly due
to those Presbyterian bank manager genes, and have always
thought that one should use things up till they fall apart before
replacing them. And I've never been huge on things like orna-
ments, or make-up, or jewellery, or the other things that feel
more like adornments, too peripheral to real life.

Yet lately I've been spending money like water, going way
beyond the necessary; getting into the positively extravagant.
Unlike my shopping habits, my over-indulging tendencies
have, thus far, always been channelled into food.
Overconsumption of the digestive sort has always been my

go-to for comfort, my greed-assuager. But maybe because the current hole I'm trying to fill is so enormous, mere food isn't coming close to satisfying it. And there is a limit, even for me, to how much I can shove in my face at any one time. So consumption of the more material sort is taking over and I'm filling my basket as I normally fill my gob – recklessly and greedily and without thought of the consequences.

What both these new behaviours – the tidying and the buying – have in common is that they satisfy a sort of nesting tendency. Often associated with new mums trying to make a comfy and safe home to bring their baby into, the nesting instinct in me seems to be about creating a safe haven for myself, filled with beautiful, comforting things, a homely home where I can breathe out, and batten down the hatches when the outside world is too upsetting and overwhelming. I'm trying to create the physical manifestation of what Bill gave me – a feeling of security, and comfort, and a feeling where my heart would lift just to know he existed. Can a lavishly, comfortably created home do that? Of course not, just as all the food in the world won't fill the hole he's left, but for now that doesn't seem to be stopping me from trying.

Therapeutic development often mirrors childhood development. People sometimes come to therapy in a childlike state of powerlessness, not knowing how to manage their lives. Over the course of the therapeutic relationship the growing emotional maturity reflects other childhood stages – via a growing independence from the therapist or mother figure – and on to adulthood. Perhaps my grieving process is following a similar path. It seems to me that what these new behaviours indicate is a move from the helplessness of childhood to the 'teenage years' of my grief when I rebel, act recklessly and, most importantly, try on new identities for size. I can't be the identity I want to be – Bill's wife – so I'm trying new selves on for size, to see who emerges in place of my old self.

~

Turns out, April IS the cruellest month, bringing what would have been Bill's fifty-seventh birthday. His best friends and I pass the evening together remembering him and mopping up each other's tears of pain and laughter.

In a reversal of the usual way of things, Bill in fact offers me a present for his birthday. The last play he wrote before he died, *Gerald*, has been chosen to open this year's INK Festival in Suffolk. I know what the play is about, but I haven't read it, so seeing it performed will be the first time I hear 'his voice' telling this story. As my train barrels towards Suffolk butter-flies correspondingly barrel around in my tummy at the thought of hearing his words and seeing the play performed. There's a particular reason why I'm nervous and haven't felt able to read it on the page. In yet another uncanny twist of fate, *Gerald* is about a widow coping with the unexpected death of her husband.

I complained earlier that one of the hardest things about grief is going through the worst, most intense, most unfa-miliar experience of my life and not being able to share it with my best friend, the person with whom I'd shared every minute detail of my day for the previous fourteen years. Every moment since he left I have wanted to tell him about how grief feels and the kind, and stupid, stuff that people say and do in response. And I can't. Well, I can – I do – but he hasn't replied.

Until now.

Watching *Gerald*, I feel that Bill does know what I'm going through, that he somehow foresaw it, and is reflecting my own experience back at me with his customary humour and keen eye for detail.

He is telling me: 'I do know what it's like; I am there with you, and I am making the funny comments that you miss hearing so much, laughing with you at the clichéd, ridiculous, insensitive things people say and do, and the kindnesses that come out of it.'

And another message loud and clear: 'What I want is for you to spend time with your friends, to laugh, enjoy life. I want you to carry on living.'

As per usual, the tears of laughter and pain co-mingle. I feel sorry for the audience members near me, not to mention the cast, who surely must hear the sobbing and feel the weight of the burden, knowing I am there watching. How he does it I have no idea, but Bill never ceases to amaze me, even – especially – from beyond the grave.

Julia Sowerbutts, festival director, asks if she can name one of INK's awards after Bill. I of course agree and the Bill Cashmore Prize for Best Newcomer is born. *Gerald*, the prize: these both feel like signposts directing me as to how to commemorate Bill in a more long-lasting way. I have an idea that has been brewing ever since the funeral, and which is now bubbling up to the surface, demanding to be acted upon.

*　　*　　*

In the October before Bill died, he booked himself onto a day-long acting course at Equity, but for some reason the course got moved to a day on which he wasn't available, and he was therefore offered a refund. Bill replied saying that he didn't want the money back; he wanted to offer his place to a student who would not otherwise have been able to attend.

I reflect on this often and it brings up so much for me. It reminds me of how generous Bill was, and how he always tried to support and encourage others, particularly those with fewer advantages than he had. This is one of those many things that manage to make me both happier and sadder at the same time. It also enrages me – I can't bear the waste of all that talent and that he never got the chance to move into a time of life when he could really follow his dreams.

But more than anything, it has given me an idea for a way that I can simultaneously memorialise him and offer hope and encouragement to others. I decide to create a scholarship in Bill's name that will offer an opportunity to disadvantaged young people to break into the theatrical world. It brings the added benefit of providing me with a project to keep me busy till I feel ready to return to work, and, just as importantly, it offers me a purpose, a solution to the existential angst that has been plaguing me.

I speak to some theatrical charities and two local theatres that Bill and I used to frequent often, and who have a good track record in supporting and developing local talent.

One of these is the Lyric Theatre Hammersmith. When I meet the team there, I know immediately that my search is over. I have found the people I want to work with. It feels right – the ethos, the people, the location; it just all fits with what I know Bill would want, and I know we can create something good here. Alongside my new colleagues there, I start plotting how to create a year-long training programme for a talented young person who would otherwise not have the resources to capitalise on their skills and ideas. This training programme will culminate in the chance to put on a full-length play or musical on the Lyric stage, thereby creating an unparalleled experience and a showcase for their work to help give them that initial foot on the ladder of a theatrical career.

I am convinced Bill would approve and knowing that helps me enormously, boosting my mood. I can hear his voice telling me yet again: 'That's the best thing you've ever done.' Had he lived, I am sure that he would have set up something similar himself one day. Sadly, the one thing we can't offer the recipients is the benefit of Bill's own fantastic teaching and mentorship, but I know his friends will offer their time and skills with his spirit in mind.

This, I believe, is a good example of rippling.

~

Irvin Yalom is an existential psychotherapist whose book *Love's Executioner* was one of the reasons I became a psychotherapist myself. His beautifully written case studies bowled me over, showing what an intricate and intimate dance is played out between therapist and client, and revealing how powerful that relationship can be.

Staring at the Sun is a more recent book, written when Yalom was in his eighties. In it he confronts his own thoughts about death, and uses his years of experience in helping clients with their death fears to come up with some interesting theories.

He talks at length about the phenomenon of 'rippling' – the notion that the things we have done in our lives, the people we have met, the person we are, all have effects that last beyond the grave. Like throwing a pebble into a pond, our lives make a big splash, the ripples of which travel far and wide, both before and after we die. Even after they have stopped being visible on the surface of the water, they nevertheless continue at a 'nano' level. The ripples may have been unconsciously created yet their effects can last for generations. Rippling seems to me to mean that we all have a shot at immortality via the impact we make while on Earth. Of course Bill's presence had massive and long-lasting effects on me, and on his friends and family, but also on those he trained, those who acted in or saw his plays or read his journalism, and even those with whom he came into brief contact but who were still touched with his kindness or humour. And we all have this capacity for immortality via our relationships and our ways of being in this world.

Bill may not have left children, but he left an awful lot else. The two theatrical legacies – INK's Bill Cashmore Prize for Best Newcomer, and the Lyric's Bill Cashmore Award bursary – are both wonderfully tangible examples of rippling, as they will allow generations of young writers, performers and directors who have never met him to gain experience, work and accolades because of him, and new creative work to appear that might otherwise not have done.

*   *   *

For me the rippling is far from 'nano', as Yalom puts it, or nuanced. Quite the opposite. The ripples from the heavy stone that was Bill's life, and the myriad repercussions of having had him in my life, are still of massive, wave-sized proportions. Some of these waves still dump me back into that turbulent ocean. But lately I find I can clamber back to the relative safety of my little canoe far more easily. And when I do, I even occasionally find that there are some waves I can actually catch, allow the canoe to be lifted onto, and surf. Even enjoy such surfing. The two awards created in Bill's name have invigorated me and given me cause for joy and a hope that I can honour him properly. More importantly, I think, they have given a purpose back to my life. I can make something good come out of his senseless death by offering something incredibly positive and life-changing to a new generation of people.

I don't yet feel ready or able to be a therapist again, but to be a mentor and a sponsor and a benefactor – that I can do, that I feel strong enough for. Thinking back to Nietzsche's 'He who has a *why* to live can bear with almost any *how*', I'm now ready to say that I do believe I may have found my 'why'.

I'm not so naïve as to believe this is an ending of any kind. The waves, both the good and the bad kind, are going to keep coming at me, and I know there are plenty of awful, dunked-back-in-the-drink days still ahead of me. Yet something is shifting. These glimmers of hope, of enthusiasm, of purpose have not been there before now. Again, I acknowledge the ever-present need to explore the boundaries of an endlessly shape-shifting grief, the need to feel into it, try each new variation on for size, and make whatever new adjustments it requires of me.

A story I read once pops up into my mind. I think it might have been another of Yalom's client histories about finding purpose. It tells of a client, an old man in his eighties, who enters therapy because he feels incapable of getting over the death of his adored wife and can see no reason whatsoever to carry on. For months the therapist struggles to help him find purpose in his misery and grief, but eventually their work together results in a realisation. He asks his client how the wife would have coped, had she been the one to outlive him. It would have been terrible, says the man, she'd have hated it. The realisation that by outliving her he has saved her having to endure the dreadfulness of grief finally provides meaning to his misery. He can see that in saving her from this pain it has purpose.

I like this thought and realise that I feel similarly about Bill. He too would have been completely distraught if I had died first, and I don't know that he would have been able to access all the support on offer from friends that I have. My years of training as a therapist have taught me one thing above all else – the ability to say 'yes please' when help is offered, rather than to revert to the internal working model I grew up with that taught me to say 'no thanks, I'm fine.' The thought of Bill having to go through what I am going through – all while potentially trying to put on a brave face as he did so – is truly horrific to me and I take comfort in knowing that I have, inadvertently, spared him this horror.

Existentialism can seem pretty nihilistic – God is dead, life is suffering and we are all going to die anyway (if I want to sum it up bluntly and reductively). Yet I have found something here that speaks to me, and feels true, and it is certainly the case that in finding a purpose, I actually feel more positive than I have for a long time. My sorrow feels meaningful and useful and I feel that, despite the chaos of the universe, through my choices I can do something about it.

And I choose, at this moment, to focus on all that Bill has bequeathed me.

When I was at the Bridge retreat I dwelt at length on all the things I had lost. It's important to do that because you can't address and come to terms with your loss without facing what exactly it is you have lost. But now I have reached a point where I can also acknowledge all that I have gained. I surely don't need to say (and yet somehow still feel the need to say) that obviously I would give up any of these gains, and more, in a heartbeat if I could have Bill back. But given that I am finally taking on board the fact that I can't have him back, no matter how much bargaining I do, nor how many futile deals with the devil I'm prepared to contemplate, I now feel ready to focus on what I do have, on what I have gained, rather than what I have lost. I want to look for any gems to be spotted among the rubble of my life and try to reframe the losses as valuable additions, ways to rebuild from the wreckage. I tell my friend Vicky about trying to focus on the positives. She comes up with a name for this concept – she calls it 'collateral beauty'. And the collateral beauty that Bill has bequeathed me consists of many things.

He has given me the idea to set up the Bill Cashmore Award, which will give me a job to do, a focus and a sense of purpose and hope. It is going to be a hugely positive force in my life and has already given me a reason for optimism and an opportunity to connect with a younger, more creative generation and a new world.

He has left me enough money to enable me to take some time off therapy work for a while, so freeing me up from the financial imperative to rush back immediately to a job that in my disordered state I don't feel up to doing. And by providing that breathing space, he has also given me the chance to start writing properly – something I have always loved doing but only dabbled in till now. And, tragically, he has given me a subject to write about – grief. And that subject, and that writing, may now be the thing that buys me yet more time away from therapy in which to recover. For I now have an agent who believes she can find me a publisher for this very book. A book that came into existence initially as a life-saver for my sanity – a way for me to get my muddled thoughts and feelings down on paper and to try to keep my therapist-self alive enough to help my grieving-self get through this. And now I'm told that it might do more, that others might benefit from reading it too. Another sense of purpose is born.

In fact, I think I'd go so far as to say that Bill set me up to survive his departure.

He did this by loving me unconditionally. Being the grateful recipient of such love, experiencing what that actually feels like, has given me greater strength, resilience and self-esteem, all of which are helping me weather this trauma.

He did this by introducing me to the Quakers, who have led me to a deeper and less inarticulate spirituality that is now supporting and comforting me.

He did this by giving me the idea to become a psycho-therapist, then supporting and encouraging me through the rigorous training. A training that gave me the theoretical and experiential knowledge to help me understand what I am going through on a cognitive level, as well as years of experience getting to know myself better so I can recognise – and alter – all my unhelpful default reactions. And above all else it provided me with a whole new raft of fantastic trained-therapist friends. Not a bad crowd to be surrounded by when hit by sudden bereavement. It's slightly uncanny how well resourced I am to get through this. But there's more.

He also set me up to survive by bequeathing me his family. At the time of his death I truly felt that Bill alone constituted my entire family, having given up on my own long ago. But now I have his family – my in-laws and their kids and grand-kids – with many of whom I have established new and lovely and supportive relationships that are not going to disappear any time soon. They made it very clear from the very beginning that Bill's death does not mean I am not still family to them. They have embraced me wholeheartedly and I love them for that. They connect me to him in a way that no one else can. They miss him as deeply as I do. And, bizarrely, his death has even rekindled relationships within my own family – it has brought me closer to my mother than I was before and enabled me to reconnect and rediscover strong bonds with some of my cousins.

Bill has bequeathed me his friends too. Most of them had also become my friends over our years together, but still I always sort of felt that they belonged to him first and foremost. Yet, just like his family, they never wavered for a moment in letting me know from the outset that I am still part of their 'tribe', that they will be there for me for good. They have honoured him by sticking with me, phoning me, adopting me as theirs, even those who I didn't know so well before his death. They have been ever-present in their concern and love for me and I have gained a new family and some amazingly nurturing relationships through them.

In fact, his death has made me completely redefine the very notion of family. I can now see that blood relations are not the be-all and end-all. I've been given the opportunity to see just how phenomenal my own friends are too. I always knew I chose well, but now that they have been tested via an unimaginable crisis, I would say we are like brothers and sisters in arms. My friendships have grown deeper and unbreakable. We have been in the trenches together, and we are surviving together.

All these people – my old established friends, those I made during my therapy training, Bill's friends and family, some of my family members – they have all formed a solid safety net beneath me and kept me buoyant.

It is not always going to feel possible to do this, but right now I am choosing to focus on the incredible good I have discovered in people, and on the unexpected delights that can emerge from devastation. I feel very blessed and grateful to have uncovered such gems from out of the rubble of my life, some sturdy planks of wood with which to fortify my canoe. I'd even go so far as to say that, viewed in this way, my leaky, wobbly canoe feels much more robust. In fact, it is beginning to feel more like a transatlantic sailboat, expertly crewed by skilled sailors in the form of my friends and family, heading towards a more focused destination – a sense of purpose.

~

Gratitude can be hard when confronted with horror, but many studies have shown that if you can spend some time focusing on the things you are grateful for, it will help bring about a wider perspective that can be useful in managing grief.

You, however, may be reading this at a time when that notion makes you want to throw things at walls, and this book in the bin. Understandable. Hold on though, if you can. I didn't say you HAVE to find gems or be grateful, and you certainly don't have to do it right now, if you are not in that space.

It can be incredibly difficult to hold two seemingly contrasting concepts in mind at the same time. How can you be furious and sad at a death, but also grateful and optimistic about an emerging, different life? Some of the more traditional grief theories suggest that in order to 'move on' you need to leave your loved one 'behind' or otherwise you will not 'recover' (how I hate that word) and will therefore be 'stuck'. Intuitively this sort of language feels completely wrong to me; in fact I can't even imagine how that could be possible. I want to enjoy my life AND I don't ever want to leave Bill behind, can't leave him behind. He is not an illness from which I need to recover but the best thing that ever happened to me. Grief is something I am learning to live with, to manage, not to mend. I am not seeking a cure, I am seeking ways to adapt and adjust to my new life without him.

Grief seems to force us ever deeper into the necessity of somehow coming to terms with living with two apparently opposing truths. That contradiction could send us mad, or it could liberate us. What if we could have both and NOT be mad or stuck? What if these two truths could be more complementary than they are contradictory? Dual process theory told us we need to look both backwards and forwards, and encouraged us to acknowledge the stressors inherent in both past and future outlooks and then to oscillate between them. But maybe as well as acknowledging the pain in both, we can also acknowledge the positives and joy of inhabiting both. I look back and am sad, but I can now occasionally also be joyful when I recall all the amazing memories and all that Bill brought to my life. And I can look forward and see fear and uncertainty, but I can also see all that remains still to live for – because I know that he would want me to, and that I can honour him and keep him alive by my doing so. Every time I feel happy I am aware of the sadness and when I am sad I also acknowledge the joy in what remains – for me, but also for him.

I feel all this intuitively – this is where my journey so far has led me, to the notion that it's okay to take him with me into the life ahead of me. A more recent grief theory has reached a similar conclusion, with years of research that reveal that others feel exactly the same as I do. We do not need to 'move on', we do not need to 'leave them behind'. We can take them with us.

~

The continuing bonds theory was put forward in the nineties by Dennis Klass, Phyllis Silverman, and Steven Nickman when they realised that the accepted prevailing notions around grief – sever ties with the dead in order to be free to make new attachments – did not accord with what their research was telling them was happening in practice.

Their continuing bonds model, based on what they were hearing in widespread research interviews, posits that instead of having to 'let go', it is in fact healthier to maintain a relationship, one that can develop and evolve alongside the griever's own developing relationship with themselves and their changed world. They say that continuing our relationship is healthy and normal and that lasting attachment is a natural, human and, in fact, *necessary* response to loss.

Instead of detaching, you can adjust and redefine the relationship to create a continuing, enduring bond, keeping the deceased with you in a way that can take account of the new you that is emerging. A living relationship doesn't remain static; you grow and change together, and so too can your relationship with your dead loved one.

The research showed many ways in which the bereaved continued their relationships – by keeping their belongings, dreaming of them, speaking to them, sensing their presence, hearing their voice even, and especially feeling watched over and being influenced by them. These are all ways in which they were sustaining their interactions and thus keeping their loved ones alive within their inner world. What also emerged was that this relationship evolved, it didn't stay the same. This was most obvious in their work with bereaved children where they saw that as the child grew, so too the relationship with the parent grew, meaning it remained age-appropriate to the child's development.

For neither of these groups does 'resolution' involve accepting and moving on. Instead their 'resolution' involves the experiences of their lost loved ones becoming part of their ongoing world.

All this research marries with what I have been feeling and doing instinctively. I still talk to Bill constantly – sometimes out loud, sometimes in my head. I feel his presence, feel him watching and guiding me. I allow him to influence my actions and my decision-making. I seek his approval and try to 'make myself more Bill', doing the things he would have done were he here. I feel a duty to ask him 'What would you do in this situation?' Consequently I find myself being more tolerant and empathic than I would have been if I weren't trying to honour his kindness and generosity. I discover that research done in the seventies by Lily Pincus showed something similar – that successful resolution often came when the bereaved identified qualities in their lost loved ones that they then incorporated into a new and adapting sense of self.

Rather than holding you back, Pincus claims, this internalisation of the dead person's characteristics and values enables you to rely less on their external presence, because you are carrying them within. Continued dialogue with this internal representation also means they do not exist as a static phenomenon, but as an ever-changing presence that can adapt as the external situation of the griever adapts and adjusts. In fact, in Pincus' description of the grieving person, her final chapter is called exactly this – Adaptation. To me this feels more realistic than the 'acceptance stage' posited by other models.

Focusing on what people actually do, as opposed to what

some think they ought to do, means old prevailing views are being re-examined. We've seen how the notion that the only way to resolve grief is to confront it head on was questioned by dual process theory. Now the concept that to resolve grief we have to disengage and leave our loved ones behind is questioned by continuing bonds theory. Common to both of these approaches is their dynamism. They allow for movement and oscillation. They recognise that grief is constantly shifting, leading us repeatedly to negotiate and renegotiate and accommodate to new scenarios, new moods and new developments.

There is a lot in Kubler Ross and Worden that I have agreed with and responded to. But to me, the newer approaches far better reflect the reality of what I have been feeling. Just as I found there to be nothing linear about the feelings and the depression and the guilt and the confusion, all of which came in all sorts of sequences, and durations, and overlaps, so too the authors of continuing bonds theory throw out all notions of stages or phases or tasks. This makes sense of why I return constantly to the feeling of being in the ocean. The ocean never stays still; it is at the mercy of the tidal pull of the moon, dragging it in and pushing it out. Even on the calmest days and in the sturdiest of boats there is movement underfoot to which you must rebalance minutely, constantly re-finding your centre of gravity. Nature isn't static and neither are we, nor our relationships.

My recurring oceanic imagery felt validated when I learned that the transpersonal approach says visualisations can be helpful in making meaning. Now it feels further corroborated by continuing bonds theory revealing that vivid imagery is particularly common in the bereavement process among widows who have been bereaved suddenly, as I was. This recognition and reflection of my own experience makes me cry. The abruptly widowed women interviewed in the continuing bonds study revealed so many things that I see in myself. They told of cognitive, emotional and somatic pain; of how much they valued their dead husbands' individuality and how they wanted to convey that to others; of how their personal identity was changing; of how concerned they were for their husbands' well-being; how strongly they felt his concern for theirs; how impossible it was to believe this concern could end with death; and, significantly, they also all reported feeling their husbands' presence. Using imagery in this way, feeling an ongoing sense of presence can, the research suggests, provide a form of internal safety. If we look back once again to attachment theory, we can see another parallel – an internalised secure base creating an anchor which enables exploration – exploration towards letting in the upsetting reality of the loss. Transformative experiences, such as those described, were able to alter and improve self-esteem. Many bereaved spouses found themselves relying on the representation of the past relationships to guide them and encourage them in their present lives.

The loss of the old me, and the consequent need for a new personal identity, is one that has dogged me since Bill died, and often thrown me completely. From that awful plane ride to St Lucia, when I went into meltdown over not knowing if I should tick married or single on their landing form, through not knowing if I could still be a therapist, not knowing if I could embrace the word 'widow', not knowing what my purpose was or who my family was, not recognising the person in the mirror who couldn't exercise, who was getting fat and old, the person who was recklessly spending lots of money and being extravagant, who was endlessly rearranging the house and its contents . . . all these things were ways of trying on and finding a new identity out of the rubble of my destroyed future.

But taking on a new identity doesn't have to mean giving up the old one; it can mean expanding on the old, adding to it, not subtracting from it. Maybe, rather than giving up the self who loves and was loved by Bill, I can keep her there, ever present in the wings, ready to bring her out on stage when we need to draw on her wisdom. And maybe I can also allow two new cast members to have the odd soliloquy or two from time to time. One newcomer is of course 'grieving self' in all her messy emotionality, whose presence on stage can still be rather erratic and unscripted. Another new cast member could be my 'Bill self', a version of me made up of all those bits of Bill I have introjected, to use the therapeutic term – the kinder, more thoughtful self that tries to emulate his better characteristics.

Chapter Six

Sailing

Summer is coming. Grateful, hopeful me sees this as another glowing gem, and is loving how the blazing sunshine and the jubilant, unstoppable, colourful blossoming of nature testify to life's fecundity and help lift my mood. But another part of me feels it differently and is forcing herself onto the stage with a contrasting message.

Something about the lightness that comes with summer, normally my favourite season, plunges me unexpectedly into yet another dark phase. I've lately found many moments of joy and gratitude, it is true, but while the sunny, long, light days are in many ways a welcome relief, signifying that the depths of the darkness are over, they are also – with the usual ambiguity of grief – a cruel reminder that I'm not actually as happy as I somehow feel I ought to be now. The summer sun reaching its apex is blinding me to all the good things that gave me such solace a few weeks ago. All I can focus on is the rubble. There is such a horrible disjunct between my internal world and the external world. When it was cold, dark and rainy outside, at least that matched how I most often felt inside. Now I feel at odds with the world around me – how can there be such beauty when my pain is so sharp? Sunshine just seems to shine a harsher light on how much better everything could be if only Bill were here. I don't often allow myself to play the 'what would we be doing if he were here now' game, but strolling alone, ice creams alone – not the same. Visiting the garden centre, or just gardening – not the same. Saying, 'Oh isn't it a beautiful day' – not the same. Doing any of those things with friends – not the same. Nothing feels as good without him. But returning home to hide from such stunning scenery causes more pain – why am I sitting inside alone on such an exquisite evening?

And worse, horror of horrors, my fiftieth birthday approaches. An event I hadn't been exactly thrilled about even when not widowed, and alone, and miserable, and terrified. It's a truly horrible age – at forty you can still sort of pretend you are relatively young and have lots of life ahead, but at fifty it is really hard to escape the knowledge that you are truly and irrevocably middle-aged. To mitigate this, Bill and I had been planning to host a massive party – a whole weekend away somewhere with all our nearest and dearest. Now, even if I felt that I wanted to celebrate, which I don't, the thought hits me – I could never organise a massive party, just for me, on my own. That feels really sad. Sad as in pathetic, not sad as in sad, but that too. I may have grown in self-confidence since being together with Bill, but I still don't feel I am enough of a 'draw' for people to want to give up a whole weekend on my behalf. Bill was the funny one, the one people would go out of their way to spend time with because he was so hilariously entertaining. And even if I could face having a celebration, Bill will not be there to make one of his hilarious speeches in my honour. I also won't have anyone to wake up with on the day itself. I'll wake up alone in an empty bed to the realisation that I am bloody fifty years old. Fifty! It sounds ancient. It's in these tiny, seemingly inconsequential, trivial even, details that the pain hits hardest.

So much for April being the cruellest month, June seems to be giving it a pretty good run for its money. Bloody summer. Bloody British people in the summer. Everything I see or do seems to trigger thoughts of yet more losses I hadn't even been aware of. Passing through a department store, I happen to walk past the barbecue section. It hits me – I will probably never host another barbecue either. It's yet another thing I'm unlikely to ever tackle on my own. Not because I'm a woman – Bill was pretty rubbish at barbecuing – just because it's not exactly the sort of event I would want to do alone. I hear people planning their summer holidays. I have nothing planned. We used to do house swaps. And here we go again. It strikes me I won't be able to do any more house swaps either – again, it's just not the sort of thing that works for one: go and pootle about in a strange house in a strange country on my own? I can't imagine anything worse. I just don't know how to make the most of things. Everything pales into insignificance without him. What's the point in nice weather?

My critical self goes to town to try to shut this sad self up. She comes in all guns blazing telling me a different sort of truth – other people manage alone, stop being so petty, just get on with life, how long are you going to milk this?

So now I feel shame at hearing my self-pitying, whining voice. Shame that nearly eight months after his death I am still having episodes like this. I always knew it had to get worse before it got better, but does it have to get this much worse? When does the getting worse stop? Is better even a thing? The platitude 'time heals' can fuck right off right now. Right now it's not healing anything, it's making it fucking worse and I've had enough of feeling worse, am sick to the back teeth of feeling worse. My old anger is reignited. Not one bubble on the cushioning bubble wrap of denial remains inflated – real life has become more insistently, relentlessly real. His absence is becoming normalised and that feels the hardest truth of all. The time since I last saw him feels vast. We've never been apart even a fraction of this time in fourteen years and I miss him with a visceral, weeping aching. Other people are forgetting him – or seem to be – and they are forgetting I am still in pain. They are assuming I am okay now because I act okay; the critical self won't let me do otherwise any more. She's terrified that others are as fed up of the whining as she is, that friends are looking for excuses to drop her and her incessant whingeing. So there are fewer public outlets for sad self to have her voice. She is only allowed out when I'm alone, and often not even then – critical self can't stand the sight or sound of her either, and shuts her up whenever possible.

I'm back in the tumultuous ocean. It's true that I have felt much more secure there recently, now that I have found my nice large yacht crewed by lovely friends and powered by a burgeoning sense of purpose, but right now we have been met by a massive storm and raging waves. I fear being swept overboard. I lash myself to a mast and pray that better weather will come before we capsize.

~

You will know by now what I believe about the individuality of grief, its unpredictability, and how there are no rules, and now I am going to break my own rule and say there is one exception, as there always should be with any good rule. And mine is this – know that there will always be relapses back into overwhelming emotions. Months, years later, however happy and together your new life has become, something will hit you – it might be obvious what the trigger is, or it might be a mystery known only to your subconscious – but it will plunge you back there; whether it be to the anger, the sadness, the hopelessness or any of the other feelings, they can and will recur. The only constant in grief – well, apart from pain – is that you will have relapses, multiple ones. Sometimes they will be quite small and short-lived. And sometimes they will feel like you have not moved on one iota, like you are right back there at the first moment of understanding.

Although this book is, has to be, linear, grief is not. It spirals and it changes shape. This book is following my journey through my first year or so of grieving, and as such it is helpful to use the passing of time as markers – from the dropping and dying of the autumn leaves when Bill too dropped and died, through the winter of abject misery and despair that followed it, via the first green shoots of spring that accompanied a tentative return to something vaguely resembling a reformatted sort of life emerging, and on to a summer of occasionally finding joy in small moments and the knowledge I'd survived. But it's not as simple and straightforward as that – I also found humour and support in the winter, pain and incomprehension in the reorganisation and otherwise enjoyable spending spree of the 'spring clean' and agony in the sunshiney blue skies of summer. Throughout it all the contradictions, the spirals and the relapses have been constantly swirling. I don't really even like the word 'relapses' – it suggests that they constitute a going backwards, as opposed to being just the latest phase along an unfolding, ever-changing (and not always in a good way) path. Perhaps a better word might be recurrences, or even just waves, because that's what they are; and like waves, they will keep coming, rendered larger or smaller by the waxing and waning of the moon of grief. Perhaps, also like waves, we need to accept and not be surprised by them; maybe one day it might even be possible to see them as a positive part of our ongoing relationship with grief.

You may be in a phase/wave of grief right now that makes this idea completely abhorrent and you just want the pain to stop and you can't be philosophical about it. That's fine. Well, it's not fine, it obviously feels horrible, and you may never want to think in this way and that's okay too, but maybe one day the thought might be useful. The recurrences, the waves – as they churn up the ocean floor they dredge up a torrent of unearthed memories of how important is the one you have lost. Don't underestimate how hard the waves hit, but maybe you could also try reframing them as part of the continuing bond, rather than something to be rid of. Or don't, if that is a notion too far for you – remember, find what works for you and don't let anyone tell you you're doing grief wrong.

It's human nature to want to structure and contain the maelstrom in neat, manageable, clearly defined stages. But remember that within this linearity there are loops. It's a game of snakes and ladders. Just look at nature to see it could not be otherwise: sometimes a sunny day bursts through in winter or a cold one in summer; sometimes a summer doesn't feel like a summer at all if the temperature barely rises, or a winter is so mild the confused flowers pop out in December. So it is with grief. Any and all of Kubler Ross's stages can come round again at any time and stay for any length of time and in any order. Any and all of Worden's tasks will need to be worked at again and again. And all of the other emotions and behaviours that haven't been swept up into list or book form, but that you may have experienced nevertheless – they too will re-emerge in the same or a different guise, possibly for the rest of your life.

And I think that is why I cling to my ocean analogy alongside my seasonal one. No one expects an ocean to be predictable. Everyone knows there are calm days and stormy ones. That waves can be gentle ripples, or fun and playful, or tsunami-sized walls of terror. Sometimes you fall out of the boat and sometimes you sail along happily till the boom hits you again, or a wave does, and you plunge back into the swell. Sometimes you swim powerfully back to the boat, sometimes you are too exhausted and sink, or if you are lucky you float. The variations are endless. I'm sure you will have your own metaphors and analogies. Mine are comforting to me; you will need to find what works for you.

So thoughts of my approaching birthday meant I fell out the boat. Big deal. It was horrible, I got wet, I hated it. But look, I'm back on board now and my family and friends are once more at the helm, getting us back on an even keel and insisting I will not spend my fiftieth alone.

*　　　*　　　*

The weekend before the dreaded day, a small group of old girl-friends from university take me to the Cotswolds for the weekend. There we pretty much do nothing but eat, drink, chat and, in suitably middle-aged style, play board games and croquet. It is a lovely, lovely weekend.

The night before the day itself Bill's sister Janey and her friend Fiona invite me out to an exhibition and supper, then stay the night with me so I wake up to a nice breakfast and some company. My friend Emma from school has lunch with me. And in the evening I'm taken out to dinner by the friends that Bill has known the longest and is closest to. We have another lovely, if somewhat subdued, evening. Hard not to be aware of the massive lack we are all experiencing. But it's great – we eat, we drink, we reminisce, we laugh, and we cry too, unable not to when we get together, those of us who have loved him most.

We say goodbye, we kiss, we hug. I walk out of the restaurant to the tube and my back seems to give out. What the hell?

I refuse to believe that my back has gone without any sort of cause or reason. I wasn't doing anything at all; I was walking completely straight, no twisting or bending or reaching, and I wasn't drunk, stumbling, or wearing high heels. It just went. I tell myself I am imagining it, it's a spasm. I get home and go to bed. I wake up in the middle of the night in pain. No, this really is a thing. It feels just like when I slipped a disc in a kayaking accident in my twenties. It is in exactly the same place and has the same sort of feel to it, but without a kayak in sight.

The osteopath confirms I seem to have dislodged the same disc. Weeks of physiotherapy ensue. I can't help but see this as a somatic reaction to my emotional state. I think my body has just told me loud and clear – on my fiftieth birthday so as to drive the point home – that however lovely it is to eat and drink and enjoy myself, there is still a massive part of me that is rebelling – against being fifty, against not having Bill, against embarking on a next chapter that will look nothing like what I had planned and hoped for the next half of my life. Back pain is seen by some as symbolic of bearing too great a weight, and maybe I just have to accept that the weight of losing Bill feels more than I can bear at this time of monumental transition into a new and unwelcome decade of my life.

But do I? Do I really have to accept this, or indeed anything? Such a problematic word, acceptance, yet this is where Kubler Ross's stages have been leading us.

~

It's autumn. We're approaching the anniversary of Bill's death. I've survived a year. I suppose it would be neat if I could end the book here with talk of acceptance and having 'done it' and how pleased I am to have got through it and how hopeful I am about negotiating the second – presumably easier – year ahead. I guess you already know I am going to resist that neat summary. Grief doesn't end, so why should this book? Well, okay, it will have to soon, I do know that, but I can't end it just yet; I need to explore its ever-changing, shape-shifting form a bit further.

I'm just not sure I can accept the word 'acceptance' either (see what I did there?), although that is where Kubler Ross's book suggests we are headed, with this as its fifth stage. For a start it's a ridiculously amorphous word that means far too many different things to far too many people. Some readings of the word are great: accept that we only have this moment, accept that things never stay the same, accept where we are right now and the sorrow and pain of what that means without resistance, accept what is in our power and what isn't. Other readings of the word are not so great – do I have to accept that it's over, stop being sad and stop all the silly talk of visualisations and messages and start dating again? God, spare me that. Continuing bonds theory, and my own experience, have already given me a pretty good notion of how to sidestep that particular reading, but for many people the word 'acceptance' is truly problematic and brings an awful lot of pressure to bear to somehow be different, to put it behind you.

Worden brings his tasks to a close with task four: 'find an enduring connection with the deceased in the midst of embarking on a new life'. That feels somewhat more 'acceptable', in that it seems to contain something of the continuing bonds notion of allowing the connection to endure while admitting that a new life is also possible. Although even there I take a bit of exception to the word 'new', which somehow doesn't allow for and include the old as being an acceptable part of the new. Maybe by welcoming in the new selves I discovered earlier, allowing them to take up residence alongside the old ones – not replacing them but letting them join the cast – maybe that constitutes my form of acceptance, how I let it make sense to me.

As usual I struggle with easy definitions or neat summaries, with words even – which remain such inadequate tools to express how complex and visceral my feelings are around this. So, I'm going to resort to a visual analogy yet again.

The Japanese have an art form called *kintsukuroi*, which means 'golden repair'. When a piece of pottery is broken, it is repaired using a lacquer mixed with powdered gold. The idea is not to ditch the pot, nor disguise its brokenness, but instead to highlight the preciousness of the wounds with the most precious material of all – gold. This putting back together and rebuilding of something shattered renders the flaws exquisite – scars to be caressed and valued. In this way a broken pot becomes a thing of new and unique beauty – a symbol of fragility but also of strength. It is transformed into a new and stunning work of art, a work of art that is different to the old pot, yet grounded in it in both shape and material, with the scar tissue not just on view, but shining forth. It allows for something beautiful to emerge from the rubble. Nothing of the original has been lost, however; it has instead been revitalised and transformed.

'Of his bones are coral made,' wrote Shakespeare, another way of saying that something beautiful can come from death. Could the grieving process even be seen in some ways as a crucible of creativity? Could 'transformation' be a more useful word than acceptance? It seems to be a word that can embody hope without the guilt, a way of allowing me to be a different version of myself while somehow keeping Bill's spirit alive and shining.

With these more hopeful thoughts buoying me up, I dare to do something I do rarely, something I still massively struggle with – I look ahead. From their habitual focus on my feet, as though on constant watch that one is still able to step in front of the other, I dare to raise my eyes and look out to the skyline. Sure enough, there on the horizon, I do spot a few glowing rays of golden hope. The light is coming through the cracks – but I can also see yet more storm clouds gathering. Here we go again. Another bloody Christmas looms.

I've always been very triggered by Christmas. I start dreading it from autumn onwards. In the early days it was the materialism that got to me most, plus the tensions within my family that always made it quite stressful. When I met Bill, we started to go away on holiday over that period and then I could enjoy it, but only really because we managed to avoid thinking about it being Christmas. When we discovered we couldn't have children it became more painful than ever, no matter where we ran to. Spending it with other people's families, those who had been blessed with children, was too painful a prospect, too much of a hammering-home of what we did not have. So we clung on to each other even more tightly and planned nice holidays instead. Not really any compensation, but at least it kept the sadness at a slightly longer arm's length and meant we had something to talk about when others were describing their big family get-togethers.

Last year's Christmas, coming so soon after Bill's death, just about finished me off, so this year I am going to steer the boat away from the gathering storm clouds in plenty of time and look for potential calmer seas. And I think I might have spied some. There is a yoga retreat in Sri Lanka that has been on my radar for quite a long time. Could this be a source of the gold needed to repair the broken pot that I have become?

Chapter Seven

Swimming

Ulpotha is a remote jungle village with no electricity, WIFI or phone signal. This tiny hamlet on a lake is home to a small community of Sri Lankans who grow their own food and run a small Ayurvedic clinic for the locals in the surrounding, equally small villages. For six months of the year the Ulpotha villagers open their doors to small groups of yogis, providing accommodation in tiny rustic mud huts within the wilderness. These huts don't have en-suites – hell, they don't even really have walls. Each consists of a raised platform of baked mud atop the jungle floor, upon which lies a mosquito-netted mattress, and above which floats a thatched roof of palm leaves held up by columns, also made of mud. Some huts have waist-high walls, some don't even have that. Either way they are completely open to all the myriad wildlife that may want to fly, slither, or clamber in. I've wanted to go there for years but Bill was never keen – far too much like camping for his more refined tastes. Now I am supremely grateful for that reluctance, because it means I can go there without having to battle a flood of memories of our having been there together. It also means, like with the skiing and horse riding that I have resolved to re-take up, I can do something that I would not have done if he were alive. Again, this is inadequate compensation of course – husband or holiday is no competition – but it is a consolation of sorts and constitutes another of those gems among the rubble that are so important in keeping me buoyant and afloat.

Another winter plane ride ensues, but this time mercifully without a landing form to provoke another existential crisis. This is followed by a long drive into the heart of the country, which provides plenty of time and space for my increasing nervousness to run rampage. What have I let myself in for? Last year in St Lucia I Skyped with friends every single day to keep me from going over the edge. This year with no WIFI or phone signal I won't even have texting options, let alone calling or Skyping as safety nets. I'm in a much better place than last year but will it be good enough? Will I sink or swim here?

First impressions, as I pad along the hard-baked red earth paths of the jungle to my remote, wall-less hut, are that it is indeed very rustic. I smile to myself as I think of how horrified Bill would have been had I ever managed to persuade him here. I doubt he would have even disembarked from the taxi. But weirdly, none of this fazes me. My nervousness falls away, and I feel at peace and content. In fact, I take to jungle life with more ease than I would have thought possible for someone born in a London suburb.

As I walk to supper an enormous full moon is shining a wide ray of light along the lake straight at me, unfurling at my feet a beautiful silver path directly to heaven. I'm determined to see this as an auspicious sign, Billy lighting my way in the most gorgeous way possible. A kintsukuroi repair in silver. I feel I am meant to be here, that I have somehow come home.

The yoga teacher is called Wade Gotwals, and he is funny and knowledgeable and creates enjoyably challenging but do-able yoga sequences. One of the many things that I like about him is that he often says, 'Move till you feel.' This is not only great yogically – the optimal way to do yoga is to go far enough that you feel like you are challenging something, but not so far that you start to get into pain – but is also a great way of negotiating grief: allow in enough to keep yourself aware of the ache of it, so that you don't descend into numb dissociation, yet also keep enough wherewithal to not go beyond what feels bearable, to know how to get yourself back from the extreme, using whatever resources you have, be that conscious withdrawal, seeking the support of friends, family, pets, exercise, food, or whatever. Replacing these two extremes with 'move till you feel' seems a perfect mantra – don't protect yourself so much that nothing shifts, but don't push yourself to the point where pain becomes torture.

Rediscovering my yogic self, alongside my daily swims in the lake, the hikes up the hills and the sleeping outdoors immersed in nature – all these things combine to bring me back into my body in a way I have missed for so long. I love it but am aware that it also brings me back into contact with something I love less – the sadness. Not a class or a hike or a night goes by without me becoming aware of the heaviness in my body and finding a few gentle tears dropping unobtrusively onto yoga mat, massage table, forest floor, or pillow.

Rather more obtrusively, they intrude in a major way during the evening practice one day when we have climbed to the top of one of the hills surrounding the lake to sit atop the flattened rock that forms the pinnacle of this particular hill. Wade leads us in yogic chanting as the sun sets over the horizon. All of a sudden, as the music flows through my newly released body, the floodgates open and I am sobbing loudly. The tears bring with them the familiar feeling that they will drown me, will never stop, and I will never be able to pick myself up again. They also bring an intense and visceral longing for Bill's physical presence, and a desperate need for a hug. Luckily the chanting pretty much drowns me out acoustically, and the descending darkness hides my contorted, snotty face. I am wishing I had brought tissues when Suzi, the manager of Ulpotha, senses into my distress and comes to put her arm round me.

Across the chanting and the darkness, Suzi has somehow tuned in to my need for connection. It is the most wonderfully simple but comforting thing: a relative stranger sensing my sorrow, and responding from a very human, empathic place. Not with words; they are not needed – and they weren't what provoked it, the music and the scenery did that – but with exactly what I do need: a fellow human touching me and acknowledging my pain. She even offers me the corner of her beautiful scarf to blow my snotty nose on. I at least have the sense to decline – I think that really goes above and beyond the call of friendship. With her help I do eventually stem the tears and descend the hill in the darkness, as always at Ulpotha, with just torchlight and moonlight to guide me.

So, much as I love it here, and I really, really do, I am finding it tough emotionally. All the physical opening, the contact with nature, and just having space to be and to think and to feel, is bringing up lots more 'stuff' I have been running from. As with the Bridge retreat, when I had a similar experience, it feels like no matter how many layers of emotion I unleash, there are always more following in their wake.

The Ulpotha tears, both the slow, gentle ones and the more violent, overwhelming ones, are accompanied by previously unearthed flashbacks that pop up unbidden: horrible memories of the hospital and those early days of trying to take it in and not being able to be left alone. I'd been doing quite a good job of keeping them at bay in recent months but now they are assailing me thick and fast. Today, swinging happily in a lakeside hammock listening to music, I am ambushed by vivid memories of a scene in the hospital that I hadn't remembered at all until now. After I had my breakdown with the organ donation team and went to say my final, final goodbye, I arrived at Bill's bedside to find the nurse in charge getting him ready for me – combing his hair and cleaning his teeth. That image feels devastating and I am unable to breathe. I am right back there in the moment and reliving it. My sobs escape me loudly and I thank goodness my hammock lies on the farthest side of the lake.

A few minutes later I hear people laughing and jumping into the lake over the other side. I have the uncomfortable realisation that sound travels easily over water. In both directions. Whoops. All those poor people trying to enjoy their relaxing holiday have just been assailed by my hideous wailing. Hopefully they assumed the unholy noise was monkeys mating or fighting. As per usual I am struck by how embedded in normal life grief is – it can't really be packaged away. I am part of the world and my grief is part of me and in the space of a minute I go from drowning in howls of agony to embarrassed worrying about being overheard. The switches are lightning quick and I am also struck by how exhausting that is, that lurch from one extreme emotion to another, from howling to shame. No wonder I am tired all the time.

~

I manage to get through a very low-key but friendly Christmas Day relatively unscathed.

Then New Year's Eve dawns and I wake up crying from a dream of missing Bill. Even here, where I feel so peaceful and happy and am having such a lovely time with such lovely people in such a lovely place, the sadness intrudes. But that is okay; I want him here with me even if it hurts. He's there in the happy moments too, I have to remember. Then it strikes me that today is the last day on which I can say 'my husband died last year.'

You hear about, and expect, the difficulty of all the 'firsts' that need to be negotiated in the first year of bereavement: the first Christmas without him, the first time his birthday comes round, my first birthday without him, our wedding anniversary, first holiday without him, first social event without him, first anniversary of his death, and so on. What I hadn't expected was all the 'lasts'. Maybe because the suddenness of Bill's death robbed me of any conscious 'lasts' as they happened, those that have come later have felt more poignant. From the biggies – like the last trip to his family home in Nottingham when I took some of his ashes to be buried alongside his mother – to the tiny things like using up the last of the shampoo that he'd bought, I have hated the lasts as much as the firsts. I thought I was done with them but now, like a punch to the stomach, I realise that this constitutes another.

From tomorrow 'my husband died last year' will become the convoluted 'my husband died just over a year ago.' I cry at how far away that makes him sound, how distant he has become, how it somehow seems to minimise the magnitude of how my life has imploded. Time might heal in some ways, but it can also deliver fresh blows. I don't want there to be this much time since I last saw him. I don't want him to recede into my past. I don't want there to be a whole calendar year's absence between us. I still don't want him gone and I'm sick of how every time I get used to his absence in one way, another way pops up to bite me that I hadn't foreseen. Today is going to be tough.

~

It is indeed a long, painful day, right up to the evening's yoga class with its end-of-year ritual. Wade asks us to write down a list of old habits or patterns that we would like to be rid of. I write down the obvious things I'd like to leave behind, like mindless eating and too much television, especially both at the same time, but I also write things like 'pretending to be okay when I'm not', which is aimed just as much at me alone as when in company. I do this because what all the yoga and the massages here are proving is that a lot of my 'okay-ness' of the last year has been no more than skin deep. I've been fooling myself along with everyone else about how well I am managing. So much of the deep, deep pain has been stored somatically in my body – in its joints, muscles and organs

– and is only now starting to release. Yesterday I had a Thai stomach massage called Chi Nei Tsang, which works on the internal organs and provoked acute discomfort and copious weeping. In the vocabulary of tears this merits the label 'painful but satisfying physical release'. All the bodywork and movement of the last few days have revealed what I have been unconsciously hiding – that the tension needed to 'hold it together' is still there, despite all the work of the last year. Deep down my body is still frozen, mummified, stuck in suspended animation, by the shock and horror of my loss. It has been held in place to defend and fortify myself from the agony. Physically I have really travelled only a very short distance, despite all appearances to the contrary.

There's no hiding now. I can't stop thinking of that extra distance, symbolically speaking, that this changing year is going to create between Bill and me. Even the hopeful realisation of how much happier and lighter I am feeling, and how much I am loving Ulpotha, is another stab wound to the heart. It shows how far I have travelled on a journey I wish I wasn't taking. I want to enjoy it, of course, and I know he would want me to enjoy it, but the fact that I am, and do, is so bitter-sweet, because it is another testament to the yawning chasm between having him with me, and me without him.

Wade's end-of-year ceremony continues. Having written down the habits we want to say goodbye to, we take it in turns to walk to the centre of the room and burn our bit of paper. I don't know exactly what my face is doing as I step up to the candle with my own list, but clearly the poker face has slipped because no sooner is the ceremony over than Suzi and another new friend, Zoe, both come to give me a hug and tell me how sad I look. 'You have friends,' they tell me. Which only makes me cry more at how thoughtful and warm these people are whom I have only known a week.

My oceanic visualisation floats back to the surface. It has been my companion from the beginning and charting its shifting nature has helped me realise how I truly have traversed an ocean. From the tsunami-like tumbling and drowning of the early days I found and clung to the flimsy flotsam and jetsam of the attempts to rebuild my life, before clambering into a leaking, rocking canoe, which gradually became a larger and more stable boat, crewed by supportive friends and bolstered by a new sense of purpose. Yet I often fell overboard or was only prevented from doing so by lashing myself to the mast. And there, I think, I have remained for months, my body responding accordingly. All this time it's been frantically gripping that mast, or the sides of the boat, knuckles turning white with the effort, body braced against the wind and the waves, trying by sheer force of will and muscle tension to keep my fragile vessel from overturning again.

I think my body has been stuck in that position for so many months that it now does not know how to let go. This yoga, swimming, hiking, massage-fest is an attempt to make the muscles release, reassure them that it is now safe enough to loosen their iron-like grip. It's working but it is bringing more pain in its wake as they learn to unfurl, and the tiredness of having held myself there for so long becomes apparent. It is that tension, that constant pre-empting of the next big wave waiting to capsize me, that the masseurs are working on releasing. I howl. As my Thai masseur digs into my kidneys, liver, spleen, I recognise that like grief, the agony is necessary – get it out, knead those knots, dig into that muscle till it lets go.

This emotive day – and year – barrels towards its inevitable end with a barbecue, a massive fire on the lakeside and a huge party where villagers and guests go wild to a mixture of Sri Lankan live bands and a Western DJ. Every time I think about it being the last day of 'last year Bill died', I feel the tears rise, but can nevertheless see and feel how very different I am on this New Year's Eve compared to last year's, and how my attitude to approaching next year is of a completely different hue to my approach to last – a year I didn't think I would survive. Yet here I am dancing, laughing, finding pleasure in my holiday, and having enjoyed, against all odds, many things from last year.

I know now that the pain and the tears and the missing him are never going to go away, but that they have changed and will continue to change flavour and shape – not always as traumatising, all-consuming and intense as during those early months, but always lurking. In some ways going forward will be worse as the missing and longing becomes more deeply felt and the physicality and proximity of him recedes, the sound of his voice fades and I get older while he does not. But I also see not only what a different place I am in, but what a different person I have become – both because of having had him, and because of having lost him.

I contemplate the beauty and the specialness of Ulpotha from amidst this joyful party, noting how at one we are – a whirling, swirling group of people aged from twenty-five to seventy-five, and from ten different countries, all surrendering ourselves to the musical blend of East and West. We are simultaneously at one with all five elements – the baked earth beneath our feet, the water of the lake to one side, the heat of the fire to the other, breathing in the warm air all around us and able to look up to the stars in the ether above.

This feels the most wonderful way to acknowledge the cyclical and individual nature of my journey, and all our journeys. The atmosphere of being so in tune with nature that prevails here cannot be created, it can only emerge through a long process of organic evolution whereby things come into being due to the concatenation of events that meld nature with the right people and the right values all at the same time. The far-sighted owners of the land who saw what this could become, the Sri Lankans whose home it is, the visitors, prepared to put the conveniences of Western connectivity to one side, whom they make so welcome, the plants, animals, birds, rain, sun, heat of the place all have to combine in a certain way and at a certain time, just as Bill and I and our friends and family combined in a certain way to create something special and unique.

I'm going to be bold and say that despite all the guilt, I do know that I gave Bill the best fourteen years of his life, as he gave me mine, and that we packed those years with more adventures than most people would have fitted into thirty years more. Bill gave me more things than I can mention while alive, and he continues to give me things that are immensely valuable in his death – self-knowledge, a more expanded world, a stronger belief in an afterlife, less fear of death, a kinder soul, a greater resilience, a vast family of love and support who have kept me going and to whom I am now irrevocably committed and will myself support to the death. The ripples continue, not just through the theatrical awards, but also in those who supported me even while they too went through the experience of losing him and who are now also forever changed by that, and by the connections we made. Just like Ulpotha's long, slow evolution, our shared experience is made up of incremental layers of love and care.

~

I've been worrying how to end this book, given that grief itself doesn't end. Chronologically the last day of the year seems a great place to finish, with me in a good place and with over a year to look back on to see how much I have changed. So I am going to draw towards a close here with the image of me dancing like a nutter round the fire by the lake. But I'm not going to make the mistake of suggesting that that is the end of it. We all want things to be resolved, to be 'better now'. But most things in life are not resolvable. We just find new ways to manage them.

My experience may ring some bells with you; you may recognise some of your own experiences in mine. But it will also be very different. You may have lost a parent, or child, or sibling, or friend, so things will be different in lots of ways. You may have also lost a spouse but possibly you had a more complicated relationship with them – maybe you argued a lot, you cheated on them or they on you, or you had maybe even been contemplating leaving them, or maybe they died after a long-drawn-out illness, or perhaps they took their own life – there are so many factors that will have made your own journey unique and will cause different responses. So you may have done many things in a completely opposite way to how I did them. You may have gone on a sexual rampage – that is another common reaction, a need to celebrate and indulge life after so much death; you may have thrown yourself into work and done lots of stunning deals, or hiked mountains, or whatever your version of success is; you might have taken to your bed for the year; or drunk yourself into a stupor; or had to, or wanted to, throw all your energies into helping your children get through the loss of their parent. The variations are again endless. I have been extremely blessed to have been in a position to be able to take an extended time away from work; others will not have had that luxury or will not have wanted that much time and space. There are so many ways to experience grief, some of which are in your control, some not.

Many people, some of my very good friends included, have found new love relatively soon after losing their partner. I am delighted and happy for those people; it is wonderful and joyful, and that is part of their journey. But it is not mine. For me that idea is still abhorrent. It may remain so, it may not – I still can't really look ahead more than a week or two, so I am not even going to speculate on whether that will be a lifelong feeling or not, and right now I don't care either way, I just want to get through the next week. Short-term thinking has served me well till now and I see no reason to change that. But what I do know, right now, is that I am pleased that the end of my story (up to this point) consists of me alone, happy and excited in many ways about the year to come.

For me, the way through grief is to develop a relationship with it. If you are alone, terrified and in pain, then use those experiences to better know yourself, to learn what you are capable of, how resilient you can be, and how love and support don't only come in nuclear-family form. They can come in friendships, old and new, in new experiences, new places, in movement and exploration and creativity and above all in connection – with others but mainly with yourself.

Grief will out. You can run but you cannot hide. And those of my friends who have children, or have found new love, have found this to be just as true for them. However happy they are with their loved ones, the pain of their loss still exists alongside their new gems, as does mine.

My happy ending is to acknowledge that there aren't really any unambiguously happy endings. Relinquishing that as a goal is a liberation and joy in itself. My happy ending consists in doing what I can to keep Bill's memory alive – out there in the wider world, as well as in my internal experience of him; it consists in finding pockets of happiness in every day, enjoying the little things that bring delight and reminders that life – albeit an unwished-for life – is still worth living. It's also about accepting the pain in every day, the moments of seeing an image, hearing a word, passing a place, smelling a fragrance that remind you of what a precious, irreplaceable person you have lost, and how desperately you miss them in your life. Even welcoming the pain as an acknowledgement of what a deep love you have lost, but knowing those moments, like the moments of joy, are fleeting and they too will pass. This is an ancient mantra – This Too Shall Pass. And everything does: the pain, the anger, the fear, the joy, the lightness, the fun, the nice people, the nasty people; like clouds in the sky they all pass eventually. We can't hang on to anything for ever – not people, not moments. All we have is now. A fairytale happy ending doesn't exist, and it certainly doesn't reside in another person. Because even if you are lucky enough to find another soulmate, they can never be him, or her, and they won't stop the loving or the longing or the missing of the one you have lost.

My own new relationship is with myself, with the new version of me. A relationship in which I hold hands with all my different internal selves, listen to them and try to give them equal time on the stage. It is also a new and evolving relationship with the non-concrete version of Bill. And it is a new relationship with my friends. I have had family redefined for me. And I have had to redefine myself: as widow not wife, alone not partnered, as receptacle for Bill's legacies and memories, and as crucible for my own emerging new self and creativity. Not better – however good anything gets, it can never be better than having him with me – but all the moping and wishing and raging and howling in the world isn't going to bring him back, and life is different. And it can be good. Not better, but different, and that can be good.

~

In this book I have tried to resist neat packaging and labels, neat interpretations and summaries – grief is too messy and

257

individual for that. But as my story draws to an end, I do feel I want to attempt some sort of a summary, even if a loosely assembled one.

My overriding impression of grief is that it plunges you deep into the terror of a world gone mad, with you mad along with it; a world where familiar structures and beliefs are blown apart, and uncertainty, chaos and anarchy reign. A world where the language you thought you knew how to speak no longer makes sense and you understand nothing. The fear of all this can cause you to desperately seek out new ways of corralling and containing this maelstrom, ways of interpreting the incomprehensible. That search for interpretation can take multiple forms and incorporate many languages.

I think this is why so many of us latch on to 'grief theories'. We hope they will offer a blueprint, a translating tool to explain and render comprehensible the chaos. As we have seen, they can indeed provide some answers to the howl for assistance we are screaming out. They can offer a path through, an easily graspable language that will guide us through the rocky terrain for which we are so ill equipped. They are useful and hold within them many truths and universals. But it needs to be acknowledged that they are just that – paths: they are not rules. As Zen teachers sometimes say, the finger pointing at the moon is not the moon. And universals may not always answer your own individual queries.

My suggestion is that it is not only in grief theories that a path or template might be found, but in therapeutic theory itself. I think it is important to look more broadly at therapeutic schools of thought, not simply those concerning grief, because our responses to grief cannot be separated from how we respond to the world in general; they affect and intersect with our own particular make-up. A bit of knowledge of what that make-up is, and what those responses are likely to be, can provide some scaffolding and resilience in the face of the onslaught.

Grief can't be packaged away as separate to real life. It is real life. We need to understand how we got to being the person we are now and why we are reacting in the way we are now because grief shows us ourselves writ large. It will either harden or strip away established ways of being. Grief renders us vulnerable to the reappearance of long-buried emotions and regressed ways of behaving. These will come to the surface and all our usual defences against having to feel these things will either be washed away by the flood or, in our terror at having to revisit things we thought we had locked away long ago, we may double down on the fortifications, a strategy that will only produce worse effects in the longer term.

Self-knowledge is the most powerful tool you have – to get through life in general, but especially to get you through grief. Therapy can be a way to provide a slightly more objective perspective on why it hurts in the ways it does. Both grief and therapy have a variety of languages with which to express themselves, ways of exploring pain, and cause and effect, and relationship, and all the other things therapy helps us explore, and which grief forces us to confront. The individuality and uniqueness of each grief journey necessarily means we all must find our own language of loss, and our own interpreter. So it is important to find which language you can most easily converse in.

Psychotherapy is one path through, a way that involves allowing a professional to be alongside us to help interpret our responses in the light of our individual way of being. But we all need more than one route, more than one interpreting tool. We each of us experience our grief in multiple dimensions and in multiple languages, not all of them verbal.

If I think about how I've personally tried to defend myself from the chaos engulfing me, it has been by cognitively engaging my brain and taking refuge in books – revisiting theory and using the language of academia to see how the great thinkers and pioneers have explained human nature to us over the years. And much has spoken to me, sometimes by validating what I have found to be happening intuitively, and sometimes simply by articulating something I couldn't grasp alone. Theory has helped me to look at my hard-wired habits, coping behaviours and defences, and my internal working models, and then helped me to challenge whether they are still useful, or are possibly now unhelpful, depending on each moment; I have found myself seeking new purpose, as suggested by the existentialists; re-establishing a grounded, secure base among my newly redefined family, as articulated by attachment theory; finding solace in thoughts of the existence of a more divine world beyond this one as explored by transpersonal theory; and by re-engaging in the movement and mindfulness that helps re-anchor me in the connection with my body, as studied by body psychotherapy.

My experience has not only been cognitive, and certainly not only verbal. I have found it, at times, very hard to articulate my experience with words, and have found my loss shouting most loudly through non-verbal means:

It has communicated via my body in pain and aching and tiredness and heaviness and other unusual sensations. And correspondingly I have had to find physical languages with which to communicate back – movement, acupuncture, yoga, cranio-sacral therapy, massage and many more.

My loss has communicated itself through the language of dreams, when my unconscious has told a different story to the one my conscious mind prefers to cling to.

It has spoken eloquently via the language of metaphor, myth, symbolism, imagery and visualisation and engulfed me in images that more powerfully convey tumultuous, inarticulable feelings.

It communicates via a spiritual language that I often struggle to grasp, and which sometimes freaks me out, yet which feels like a powerful communication nonetheless.

It communicates via the age-old means of storytelling as a way of meaning-making. I have felt the need to express my pain out loud, to summon up some creativity and write this book.

I have tried to interpret and tell the story of my losses in these many different languages, as you will have to tell yours in yours.

~

Midnight is getting closer. The Ulpotha fire and the frenzied dancing have made me hot and sweaty. I plunge into the lake for a moonlight swim to cool off. As I swim I see where my oceanic visualisation has been leading. I can now choose to plunge into the water of my own accord, and of my own free will. When there I can feel empowered not lost, joyful not terrified. As I swim, I feel in control and happy to be in this moment, to have chosen water to be my friend not my foe. As I use my own agency to power my way through, I am in tune with this soothing water, not battling it. Yet I remain mindful of its ultimate dominion. I know the damage it can do, but I also know that I can master it – at times. And at this particular time, feeling at one with nature, I can use it for my own ends, to tone my muscles, cool my body temperature and calm my mind. But there will be other moments when I will veer off course and get a bit tangled in the lily-pad stems, or occasionally someone might float past on a canoe, causing a little ripple in the water so I have to recalibrate; but I know that I can ride these waves without fear, that I can stay afloat, and that there is a boat waiting for me to clamber into when I tire.

The journey isn't over, but it does have different scenery, and a different feel. And my love for Bill is different. Just as it changed and grew as we grew – from when I first met him, to how it was five years in to our relationship, ten years in, fourteen years in, and now after his death. The love never wavers but it adapts. And that's because we all change and grow as people, and my love for him will continue to change now, as I change, because I cannot and don't want to stay the same. The love won't lessen, but it will adapt to my new situation. And Bill would want me to change and to live my life in the way that best suits me now; I have no doubt at all about that because all he ever wanted was my happiness and he devoted his life to that end. I owe it to him to try to be happy, when I can. Anything less would be a betrayal. I know he is cheering me on and will be coming with me on the next stage of the journey, wherever that leads. I'm not leaving him behind; he's coming along as part of me, giving me inspiration and courage and strength and creativity and kindness. And I will die a better person for having known him and for having loved him in life, and in death.

Over on the shore I can hear the countdown to midnight starting. As I float on my back, held lightly by the water beneath me, I look up and see fireworks exploding over the lake, lighting up the night sky. I feel I finally know how to end this book. I think back to the eulogy I gave at his funeral:

> I am heartbroken. But I am not broken – and that I am able to say that is entirely due to Bill – I am stronger now than when he met me all those years ago, and that is because I have had fourteen years of being loved unconditionally by a man with the biggest heart I know. Bill, marrying you is the best thing I have ever done.

As Bill's familiar refrain of encouragement rings in my ears, I know that the coming year will bring waves of pain when I think of the happiness I have lost. But I also know that, like the ebb and flow of the water beneath me, it will bring waves of new happiness I am yet to discover too. And Bill will be alongside me for both. He still represents my safe ship of stability, and will be sailing with me on to the new adventures and uncharted seas ahead.

Acknowledgements

I couldn't have survived this last year, much less written a book about it, if it wasn't for my unbelievably kind, loving and supportive friends. So many people have rushed to my rescue, even while in the midst of their own grief, and I will be eternally grateful to all of them. I love and want to say thank you, from the bottom of my heart, to these extraordinary human beings:

Ellie Bates, Chris Bilton, Dolly Clew, Julia Cooke, Katie Dias, Libby Davies, Broo Doherty, Jess Fawkes, Sarah Fielding, Sandra Gillespie, Jonathan Gough, Tamsin Greig, Louise Hooper, Tanya Hudson, Simon Marlow, Tim Marlow, David Murray, Claudia Nella, Mariana Panayides, Andy Powrie, Sherie Ryder, Inge Samuels, Nicole Scott, Peter Sweasey, Mike Sims, Zephyr Wildman, Polly Woodford, Anya Woolliams, Kerri Wright, the Charlton, Rowe, and Cashmore families, and to Hammersmith Quakers.

I would also like to thank my wonderful agent, Jane Graham Maw, for taking a punt on an unknown author, my publisher Liz Gough – ditto – and my editor Jacqui Lewis.

And, most importantly of all, I would like to thank Bill Cashmore for giving me the best fourteen years of my life, and for installing in me the courage and confidence that has enabled me to keep going in his absence.

About the Author

Sasha Bates is a psychotherapist, journalist and former documentary filmmaker. Eighteen years in the TV industry saw her write, direct and produce series as varied as *Omnibus, Grand Designs, Live and Kicking,* and *How to Look Good Naked,* alongside an ongoing side-line in travel journalism.

Her fascination with people – and what creates the myriad dynamics between us all – fuelled her career as a filmmaker, and she discovered a need to understand the human mind, emotions and relationships. She left television behind and re-trained as an integrative psychotherapist, gaining an MA, a Diploma in Counselling and an Advanced Diploma in integrative psychotherapy from The Minster Centre in London. Once fully qualified, and after stints working in the NHS and in higher education, she started up in private practice where she gained a reputation as an embodied therapist, an earlier training as a yoga teacher having given her a good understanding of the mind body connection.

When her husband, Bill, died unexpectedly at just 56, Sasha turned back to writing to help her navigate the new and unwelcome world into which she had been thrust. She now teaches workshops about grief to therapists, and to other grievers, and has set up a commemorative theatrical bursary – The Bill Cashmore Award – in conjunction with the Lyric Theatre Hammersmith.

To find out more and to donate please visit:
www.sashabates.co.uk/bill-cashmore-donation
www.billcashmore.co.uk